*Conventional Wisdom*

CB

# Conventional Wisdom

*The Content of Musical Form*

Susan McClary

UNIVERSITY OF CALIFORNIA PRESS

*Berkeley   Los Angeles   London*

Library
University of Texas
at San Antonio

University of California Press
Berkeley and Los Angeles, California

University of California Press, Ltd.
London, England

© 2000 by the Regents of the University of California

Library of Congress Cataloging-in-Publication Data

McClary, Susan.
    Conventional wisdom : the content of musical form / Susan
McClary.
        p.   cm.—(Ernest Bloch lectures)
    Includes bibliographical references and index.
    ISBN 0-520-22106-0 (alk. paper)
    1. Music and society.   2. Tonality.   3. Blues (Music)—
History and criticism.   4. Postmodernism.   I. Title.
II. Series.
    ML3795.M35   2000
    780—dc21                                          99-29428
                                                         CIP


Manufactured in the United States of America

08   07   06   05   04   03   02   01   00

10   9   8   7   6   5   4   3   2   1

The paper used in this publication is both acid-free and totally
chlorine-free (TCF). It meets the minimum requirements of
ANSI/NISO Z39.48-1992 (R 1997) (*Permanence of Paper*).

*To my mother, Toccoa Wilson McClary—*
*my first and best source of conventional wisdom*

# TABLE OF CONTENTS

# PREFACE

As soon as Joseph Kerman telephoned to invite me to deliver the Bloch Lectures at the University of California at Berkeley, I started casting about for a suitable project—one that would best take advantage of the public platform offered by this distinguished series. It took me quite a bit of time to weave the various themes treated in *Conventional Wisdom* into a coherent pattern. But my first priority—the one around which all the others coalesced—was to find a topic that would allow me to move easily between European art music and popular repertories.

I doubt that this is what Joe had expected. My name was most closely identified at the time—and probably still is today—with projects concerning gender, and the chapters that follow testify to the fact that they were written by a feminist. But feminism has always counted as only one of my interests. At a far deeper level, all my work addresses questions of musical signification—in particular those aspects of musical practice that seem so natural as to elude observation. This is why even the essays in *Feminine Endings* invariably came around to focusing on formal procedures and tonality. For it had seemed when I was writing *Feminine Endings* that the (to me) self-evident representations of gender and eroticism I was tracing would reveal the complicity of these basic formal principles in a variety of culturally specific agendas, thus enabling a thorough historical reassessment of these elements.[1]

I should have anticipated, however, that the attention of the discipline would fixate on the scandals of gender and sexuality themselves. Or, in the words of Madonna, "Oops! I didn't know I couldn't talk about sex (I musta been crazy!)."[2] Moreover, because much of the music I examined in *Feminine Endings* participated in or operated in deliberate opposition against the somewhat sexist enterprise that most culture has been, my demonstrations took on a pessimistic tone not characteristic of much of my other work. As a result, I became widely identified as a basher of Western culture.

Yet my principal critical concerns date back to my work on seventeenth-century Italy. I became increasingly dissatisfied with the accounts of early music available when I was in graduate school in the late 1960s, and I sought to find ways of explaining—to myself, if to no one else—how music of the 1600s "works" (whatever *that* means, as my exasperated mentors lamented). Because I could find no models that shared my ways of thinking or hearing, I had to cobble together my own methods from old modal treatises and score study. From the outset of that project, it seemed clear to me that I had to learn to resist the easy solutions my tonal theory training had given me. To be sure, tonal analytical devices allowed me to label chords; but when I had finished attaching my Roman numerals, I found that my perplexity had only increased. What I was seeking could not be discovered as long as I littered the score with ready-made but inappropriate tags. By the time I finished my dissertation, this habit of disallowing tonal answers had become so ingrained that I no longer took "tonality" as something already understood, even when I dealt with eighteenth-century music.

But I soon experienced what felt like a catastrophic professional setback, as journals sent my dissertation-based articles back to me with the condescending explanation: "You don't seem to understand: music of this period can't be analyzed because its composers hadn't figured out yet how music should go." Now recall, if you will, that I wasn't working with what musicologists like to call a *Kleinmeister* (nasty term!) but with Claudio Monteverdi, whom I thought we counted among the biggies of all time. Silly me! (Oops! I didn't know I couldn't talk about modes!)

After having run through most of the professional journals with much the same response, I decided that before I could do my seventeenth-century work in peace I would have to make explicit the cultural premises that underlie the music that "works the way music is supposed to work."[3] And that meant placing in their respective historical contexts the music of Bach, Mozart, Beethoven, Schubert, Tchaikovsky, Brahms, Schoenberg, and so on and so forth. Alas! If the Powers That Be had agreed to publish my innocuous little articles on mode, I might be contentedly analyzing Obrecht now.

While I was in the midst of this now-notorious rereading of the standard repertory, I also came into contact with feminist and cultural theory. Moreover, I began listening to the popular music that I had always avoided for fear of immediate professional death. These enterprises—feminism, cultural theory, popular-music studies—are very different from each other, yet together they reinforced the urgency of my original agenda and encouraged me to explore genres I never would have anticipated. Along the way, I became persuaded that our difficulty in telling a coherent history of music in the twentieth century stems in part from our refusal to acknowledge one of the most important facts about culture of the last hundred years: namely, that the innovations of African Americans have become the dominant force in music around the globe—universal in ways Kant could not even have begun to imagine. But dealing with these other kinds of music also requires different sets of approaches—ones that engage with musical specificity without trying to stuff pieces into irrelevant formal criteria.

The Bloch Lectures gave me the opportunity to focus on the broader philosophical issues that had driven my work. Many of these issues have only gradually become apparent to me, sometimes only after I inadvertently stumbled over a tripwire that triggered unexpected reactions. Thus projects that would seem to have nothing in common—the analysis of a madrigal from 1604, the examination of sexual politics in Richard Strauss's *Salome*, the discussion of harmonic strategies in Laurie Anderson's "O Superman"—have produced responses that sent me back to the same basic set of questions: how can we talk about meaning in musical procedures?

I have chosen to retain as much as possible the discursive quality of the original lectures in this book. Although I have expanded the texts of the five hour-long talks a bit, I wanted to maintain the sense of interconnection among the chapters rather than allowing each to become the book-length study it obviously deserves. But I hope the ideas that emerge from my assemblage will justify its odd juxtapositions and compensate for its more-than-occasional sketchiness.

I focused in each of the Bloch Lectures on at least one and often several pieces of music—a relatively simple thing to do in a live presentation but a rather more difficult feat to pull off in the format of a book. Because many of my examples in the final chapter still have considerable commercial value, it has proved prohibitively expensive to collect them into a single CD for the reader's convenience. Yet the discussions throughout the book will make little sense in the absence of the sounds they attempt to interpret.

Fortunately, most of the pieces featured in the book (with the exception of the arias by Stradella and Scarlatti, both of which appear here in score) are reasonably easy to find in libraries and record stores. In putting the lectures together, I sought to draw together a wide variety of dazzling tunes—tunes that ordinarily would not show up in the same context—and the resulting sonic montage is itself a crucial part of the project. Consequently, I urge the reader to take the trouble to locate and listen to the music along the way; anyone who does so will have the reward of experiencing directly these extraordinary repositories of conventional wisdom.

I wish to thank Joe Kerman for graciously inviting me to Berkeley in 1993: it is humbling to be deemed worthy of inclusion in a series of such distinguished composers and scholars. My visit was greatly enriched by conversations with Barbara Christian, Jocelyne Guilbault, Barbara Laslett, Tony Newcomb, Richard Taruskin, Bonnie Wade, and the challenging students in my graduate seminar on postmodernism. I have also benefited from the careful readings of these chapters by Joe Kerman, Larry Kramer, Roger Bourland, and José David Saldívar. Although I did not bother Philip Brett, George Lipsitz, Richard Leppert, Chris Small, or Rose Subotnik to read drafts of the book, they stand as my models for their ethically grounded interdisciplinary work on music.

I also wish to thank McGill University, which granted me a leave so that I could teach at Berkeley in spring 1993. My Montreal colleagues and students lent unconditional moral and intellectual support, and I miss them (if not their climate) very much. I also received invaluable comments from the faculty and students at McMaster University—especially Jim Deauville and Susan Fast—when I delivered some of these talks as the Hooker Lectures there in 1994.

Two years after I delivered the Bloch Lectures, I was the happy recipient of a MacArthur Fellowship. Unfortunately, I had just signed on to chair my department at UCLA, which made taking sabbatical leaves impossible for three years. On completion of my term of office, I was at last able to return to the lectures and to convert them into this book. I am grateful to the MacArthur Foundation and to UCLA, both of which have supported me while I continued my research and revisions. Additional thanks go to Dean of Humanities Pauline Yu, who made it possible for me to acquire the very best colleagues anyone could hope to have: Mitchell Morris, Elisabeth Le Guin, Raymond Knapp, and Robert Fink have not only aided and abetted me in my work but also have made the musicology corridor of Schoenberg Hall a hotbed of intellectual ferment and good times. I also owe a great deal to my students at UCLA—particularly David Ake, Paul Attinello, Steven Baur, Stuart De Ocampo, Marischka Hopcroft, Maiko Kawabata, Jacqueline Warwick, Thomas Willmann, and Nadya Zimmerman—who have helped me hone my thoughts and who continue to goad me on to new ideas. They remind me on a daily basis why the whole enterprise of music study is worthwhile.

I owe more than I can express to my editors at the University of California Press—especially Doris Kretschmer and Lynne Withey—who encouraged me every step along the way and who helped me to hack this book into shape. They and my colleagues on the UC Press Editorial Board have constituted my favorite academic community over the course of the last three years.

My toughest critic remains Robert Walser, who enabled me to keep going with the project while insisting that it measure up to his impossibly high standards. But more than that, his influence permeates this book: I could never even have imagined such an enterprise without the continual questioning of cultural hierarchies our marriage (heavy metal and jazz meet modal theory and Mozart) has demanded of us. We have listened together to thousands of tunes—early music from my camp, the whole range of popular musics from his—and discussed how best to account for their powerful effects. When we met in 1984, I still mostly aspired to earn the professional title of Miss Mode; that I could have ended up writing a book like *Conventional Wisdom* testifies to the extraordinary impact of Rob's vast musical knowledge, his scholarship, and the pedagogical patience with which he has introduced me to the pop music I managed somehow to miss while growing up. 'Nuff said.

But I could never have written the lectures themselves without daily infusions at the Roma coffeehouse on Ashby and College. Keep the lattes flowing!

# Chapter 1

# Turtles All the Way Down
# (On the "Purely Musical")

An old legend tells of an earnest youth who went to a holy man seeking the meaning of life. In response to the disciple's questions about the world and its foundations, the guru explained that the earth sits on the back of a huge tiger, which stands on the flanks of an enormous elephant, and so on. When the cosmological series reached a giant turtle, the sage paused. His enraptured pupil—believing he had arrived finally at ultimate truth—exclaimed, "So the universe rests on that turtle!" "Oh, no," replied his mentor. "From there, it's turtles all the way down."[1]

I often find myself reflecting on this story as I experience the tensions between my work and the work of many others in my discipline. Over the course of the last fifteen years, I have engaged in what might appear to be a wide range of unrelated projects; yet in all of them, I have sought to explore the social premises of musical repertories. This fundamental concern motivates not only my accounts of how gender-related issues have intersected with music at different historical moments but also my studies of narrative strategies in Mozart or Schubert and my attempts at making sense of today's popular culture.[2]

Of course, I am not alone in my quest for cultural interpretations of Western art music. Indeed, the numbers of those concerned with such matters have increased to the point where we are now widely known (for better or worse) as "the New Musicology." My colleagues in this endeavor include (most prominently) Rose Rosengard Subotnik, Lawrence Kramer, Richard Leppert, Philip Brett, Gary Tomlinson, Richard Taruskin, Robert Walser, and—the godfather of us all— Joseph Kerman, whose calls for music criticism and attacks on the "purely musical" date back several decades.

Yet despite the growing number of scholars committed to cultural interpretation and regardless of which project I happen to be pursuing, I continue to meet resistance from those who claim that most aspects of music—indeed, the ones that really matter—operate according to "purely musical" procedures. For while we all might agree that elements such as Baroque word-paintings or eighteenth-century *topoi* are referential, many musicologists and music theorists still like to assume that these elements simply perch on the surface of what underneath is autonomous bedrock. No gender, no narratives, no politics: just chords, forms, and pitch-class sets. And the discussion stops there.[3]

But those moments at which the investigation gets arrested have always intrigued me more than any others. Why does tonality emerge when and as it does in the seventeenth century? Because of "natural" evolutionary processes. Why does a sonata movement require that its second theme resolve into the key of the first? Because that's the way musical form works; end of conversation. But WHY? Like an unsatisfied child, I have pressed on beyond those limits to know more. And like a jaded culture critic, I have found it impossible to accept any kind of bedrock certainty, anything natural or purely formal in the realm of human constructs. Whichever position I take—that of child or culture critic—I always return to the conviction that "it's turtles all the way down."

Musicologists do grudgingly acknowledge one cluster of turtles: we refer to them as conventions. By "convention" we usually mean a procedure that has ossified into a formula that needs no further explanation. Why does a minuet repeat its opening section following the trio? Convention. Why do pop ballads end with fade-outs? Convention. Why did thousands of males undergo the knife in order to sing in the soprano range in Baroque opera? This last question—posed year after year by incredulous undergraduates in their music history surveys—is typically answered with the strangely threatening tone of voice parents reserve for inquiries about the Primal Scene: IT'S JUST A CONVENTION! Which translates—Don't ask.[4]

Since the nineteenth century, Western art has cultivated an aversion to conventions: we commonly exalt as "purely musical" the procedures that appear to have transcended signification, and we scorn conventions as devices that have hardened to the point where they no longer can mean anything at all. Thus, we have, on the one hand, patterns that operate beyond the petty concerns of cultural meaning and, on the other, clichés emptied of whatever communicative power they might once have possessed. We interpret reliance on convention as betraying a lack of imagination or a blind acceptance of social formula.[5] In either case, the individualistically inclined artist or critic shuns them with disdain and seeks value in those moves that escape the coercion of convention—that aspire, rather, to the condition of the "purely musical."[6]

Yet at the same time, we make concerted efforts to locate regularity within precisely those compositions that seem to have managed to escape the bounds of normative practice. The measuring sticks of Schenker graphs or the kabbalistic methods of set-based analysis strive to pull apparently unruly music back inside the horizons of the rational, the orderly, and (implicitly) the metaphysical.[7] Why, I have always wondered, do we not label the procedures such theories trace likewise as conventions? And why do we neglect to talk about why these procedures matter so very much to us?

In this book, I want to claim that this split between conventions and the "purely musical" is itself socially and historically contingent, that the procedures we regard at different moments as "purely musical" count rather as the most crucial set of conventional practices. I will scan through various stacks of turtles, sometimes teasing out the complex functions served by obvious conventions, sometimes addressing those clearly referential elements perched on the surface, sometimes prying into the shells of "purely musical" processes to examine their ideological premises. And while these turtles may occupy a range of positions within their respective stacks, I will not treat them as different in kind. No metaphysics—just cultural practice. Nothing but turtles. All the way down.

The periods in musical style that stand out for consistency in procedure—for example, the High Renaissance, the late eighteenth century—are those for which the hierarchy is at its most stable, though for a wide variety of historical and cultural reasons. If we remain exclusively within the domain of a particular style, we might well come to accept the premises characteristic of that repertory as Truth, just as our young disciple wanted to regard the giant tortoise as a *terminus ad quem*. We are less likely to do so, however, if we have witnessed the moments when the dominant turtles first slipped into those privileged positions and when they slipped back out again. During other times— for instance, the early 1600s or the late 1990s, the subject of Chapter 5—the scrambling is rather more apparent: an expressive device might become a standard procedure, a convention might be revived for use as a surface signifier, and so on. This is why I prefer in my work to take a rather wider view of history. For the jostling among expressive devices, conventions, and "purely musical" procedures becomes most apparent during those episodes of stylistic flux.

Enough of turtles for now, however. Even if we do not commonly approach music from this point of view, my project resembles several lines of inquiry long central to cultural studies and literary theory, including the work of Hayden White, to whose *The Content of the Form* I pay homage in my title.[8] I want to explore in music history the kinds of processes Raymond Williams calls "structures of feeling," Fredric Jameson the "political unconscious," Roland Barthes "mythologies," Thomas Kuhn "paradigms," Kaja Silverman "dominant fictions," or Ross Chambers simply the "social contracts" that establish the conditions for the production and reception of artworks.[9] Whatever we label these structures, they are intensely ideological formations: whether noticed or not, they are the assumptions that allow cultural activities to "make sense." Indeed, they succeed best when least apparent, least deliberate, most automatic. Although musicologists and theorists often grant these kinds of formations the status of the "purely musical," I will treat them as conventions—albeit conventions that so permeate human transactions that we usually fail to notice their influence. And I want to examine the values they represent, the interests they reinforce, the activities they enable, the possibilities they exclude, and their histories within the contested field that music inevitably is.

I have chosen my title, *Conventional Wisdom*, for two principal reasons. First, the phrase itself is a convention, a cliché that refers to commonly held but wrong-headed beliefs. We use it rhetorically to set up a surprising item of information: conventional wisdom has it that X; but in point of fact—Y! Just hearing the words "conventional wisdom" prepares us for that rude reversal, whereby something that seemed to have possessed truth-value gets relegated to the scrap heap of superseded misconceptions. Schoenberg's refiguring of tonality in his *Theory of Harmony* and Monteverdi's *seconda-prattica* manifesto both adopt something of this tactic, as they explain why the apparently universal laws of syntax they had inherited were "merely" conventions, why they felt free—even obligated—to push them aside.[10] My title draws on that same ironic stance, for I will seek to redefine what conventional wisdom has elevated as the "purely musical" to the status of social contract.

Yet my title also means to acknowledge the fact that genuine social knowledge is articulated and transmitted by means of shared procedures and assumptions concerning music. I want to insist that a great deal of wisdom resides in conventions: nothing less than the premises of an age, the cultural arrangements that enable communication, co-existence, and self-awareness. At the same time, none of them counts as anything more than artificial constructs human beings have invented and agreed to maintain—in particular contexts, for particular reasons, to satisfy particular needs and desires.

Consequently, conventions always operate as part of the signifying apparatus, even when they occupy the ground over which explicit references and encodings occur: in other words, it is not the deviations alone that signify but the norms as well. Indeed, the deviations of particular pieces could not signify if we did not invest a great deal in the conventions up against which they become meaningful.[11] Thus, while the traditional methods of hermeneutics often focus on explicating deliberate meanings, my project also factors in these seemingly automatic dimensions—which I take to be the most crucial because the most fundamental. In addition to paying attention to what individual compositions articulate on their surfaces, I will also examine the frames within which their strategies make sense as human endeavors.

The old question of form versus content has long been criticized as presenting a false dichotomy, especially perhaps in music. Theorists since the nineteenth-century critic Eduard Hanslick have generally solved the split by redefining everything as structure—thus the institutional prestige of our graphs, charts, and quasi-mathematical explanations of music. The more we have placed our trust in rigorous, self-contained analysis, the more we have had the impression that we might eventually explain it all on the basis of idealist abstractions.[12]

But too much is left out of such accounts, for the course of music history never did run smooth: the anxieties produced by collisions between incompatible practices or by the oedipal struggles between successive styles always involve far more than just notes. Plato warned that "the modes of music are never disturbed without unsettling of the most fundamental political and social conventions."[13] The power of music—both for dominant cultures and for those who would promote alternatives—resides in its ability to shape the ways we experience our bodies, emotions, subjectivities, desires, and social relations. And to study such effects demands that we recognize the ideological basis of music's operations—its cultural constructedness. Even the urge to explain on the basis of idealist abstraction or to insist on an unbridgeable gap between music and the outside world stands in need of explanation, an explanation that would require a complex social history stretching back more than twenty-five centuries to Pythagoras.[14]

Thus, in contrast to Hanslick's resolution in the direction of form, I want to treat the entire complex as content—social, historically contingent content. As Adorno puts it, "Form can only be the form of a content."[15] Moreover, I will claim that music (like other kinds of human artifacts) is assembled of heterogeneous elements that lead away from the autonomy of the work to intersect with endless chains of other pieces, multiple—even contradictory—cultural codes, various moments of reception, and so on. If music can be said to be meaningful, it cannot be reduced to a single, totalized, stable meaning. At the same time, its polysemousness does not justify our long-standing avoidance of interpretation. For if music frustrates our attempts at nailing down definitive meanings, it does so no more than poems, films, or paintings, all of which maintain a considerable degree of indeterminacy.

As even readers with little investment in what is called "postmodernism" have already no doubt discerned, my project shares many of the deconstructive assumptions animating much of the current work in literary criticism and film studies. Like similar investigations in those other disciplines, this book will strive to take apart into their constituent elements many of the procedures we have embraced as "natural." Yet my project differs tactically from that of most literary theorists.

Meaning has long seemed too immanent in verbal language. Accordingly, practices such as deconstruction strive to draw our attention to the opacity, constructedness, and undecidability of texts, literary and otherwise. But music studies have a different history—one that has long denied signification in favor of appeals to the "purely musical," that places music beyond the reach of "mere" social arrangements. And this history of denial, I would argue, has put us in what is no longer a tenable position for our understanding of musical cultures, either past or present. Thus before we can properly embark on programs that seek to destabilize musical signification, we have to recover some notion of how musical gestures, procedures, and forms do, in fact, produce their very powerful effects.[16] Otherwise we simply hop from one brand of skepticism to another without ever having to consider how music actually operates as a cultural practice.

This book pursues what might appear at first a rather circuitous logic. Following this introduction, the second and third chapters deal respectively with the two conventional schemata that have contributed most to the formation of our musical world today: first the blues, which has provided the basis for so many genres of African American and popular musics throughout this century; and next that European convention most often regarded as "purely musical"—namely, tonality. Chapter 4 examines what happened in the nineteenth century when conventions became anathema, when artists took flight from the faintest whiff of preordained behavior.

In the final chapter, I explore some aspects of the current musical scene, in which several long-dispelled conventions have returned home to roost. Indeed, to a great extent, the present moment and our difficulties as musicologists in making sense of it have shaped this entire book. It is the urgency of our predicament that led me to study the blues seriously, to reflect on European culture's investment in tonality, and to explore alternative ways of understanding the course of music history.

If I want to reject the possibility of the "purely musical" and to reassign those elements so often exalted as "purely musical" to the realm of convention, I also expect to reinfuse all these levels—whether expressive devices, explicitly conventional formulas, or deeply buried assumptions—with meaning. Not, to be sure, the giant turtle of transcendental meaning or even consistency; but human meanings, grounded in the historical contexts in which they performed—and, in many cases, *still* perform—crucial social functions. If in the final analysis we have nothing but turtles, our turtles ought to suffice.

I want to begin by examining two pieces of music, both of which reside slightly outside what we commonly regard as conventional practices— far enough outside, in any case, that we cannot simply lunge for accounts based on formula yet close enough that we may be able to detect *as such* some of our usual habits of listening as they are engaged or frustrated.

My first example comes from the oratorio *La Susanna* by Alessandro Stradella, the foremost Italian composer of dramatic music between Francesco Cavalli and Alessandro Scarlatti.[17] According to the scriptural source—the Book of Susanna in the Apocrypha—Susanna is a virtuous young wife, entirely above reproach. Yet her beauty has enflamed two elders of the community. They hide in her garden, spy on her as she bathes, then accost her—threatening to testify that they caught her in the act of adultery unless she submits to their desires. When she refuses, they indict her, knowing full well that the penalty for adultery is execution. Just as the authorities prepare to stone her, the young prophet Daniel steps forward, interrogates the elders separately, establishes their mendacity, and thereby saves Susanna's life and reputation.

The schematic good-versus-evil narrative presented in the Apocrypha never suggests that Susanna compromises her chastity. Yet during the Renaissance, her story became the justification for a whole genre of paintings that depicted her nude, often brazenly displaying herself. Those viewing these paintings could feast their eyes on her beauty, secure in the knowledge that the scriptures themselves legitimated the subject of their gaze. Stripped of the narrative that ultimately redeems Susanna, this excerpted moment panders to latter-day stand-ins for the elders. With Daniel removed from the picture, she is positioned as Diana without Acteon's hounds to defend her honor. Moreover, artists often fuse her representations with the iconography traditionally associated with *Vanitas*, making her seem to anticipate and, consequently, to condone the elders' lust as she gazes into a mirror in autoerotic rapture.[18]

Stradella's oratorio (libretto by Giovanni Battista Giardini; Modena, 1681) spends considerable time with the elders—both depicted as the stock aging lechers of commedia dell'arte—before he introduces Susanna herself. The elders exchange boastful metaphors, each claiming greater degrees of arousal, then hide together in the bushes to wait for her arrival at the bath. As if their locker room buildup were insufficient to eroticize Susanna's entry, the *testo* or narrator—a cross, in this case, between the evangelist in a Bach passion and a leering MC like Joel Grey in *Cabaret*—describes with Marinesque language dripping with double entendres her cruel progress to the pool (she crushes the grateful, masochistic grass under her feet), the lily whiteness of her breasts, the purple of her lips (envied by the roses as they look up at her from beneath), and the rapturous gushing of the fountain's deities when she lowers her naked body into their waters. Our attention—the gaze of the ear, which has to suffice in this unstaged genre—is drawn inescapably to the libidinal as Giardini's poetry eroticizes her every fiber before she even opens her mouth.[19]

Moreover, Stradella's music marks the recitative with sudden chromatic relocations of key that continually raise the erotic stakes. The testo seals off his discussion of the elders in D minor, just before this passage. But three times over the course of this short speech he shifts abruptly by a major third to a new key only distantly related to the one to which we had become accustomed (D to B♭, E♭ to C, C to E). This device has the effect of canceling out the previous tonality and asserting another: a series of maneuvers that simulate a quick succession of phenomenological states. Winks and nudges? Progressive degrees of arousal? The effect depends on the performance, but it in no way counts as a neutral setting.

Following this buildup, the apocryphal heroine at last receives a full scene to herself—albeit a scene hedged around by interlopers both on the stage and in the audience. Her *scena* opens with an aria in which

Susanna—in her fateful bath—contemplates God, her devotion, and (significantly) her unworthiness. Because this is her first utterance in the oratorio, the aria sets the tone for her characterization (Ex. 1.1).

> Quanto invidio vostro stato,
> Care limpide sorgenti.
> E'il mio cor contaminato,
> E voi siete acque innocenti.
>
> How I envy your condition,
> Dear limpid springs.
> My heart is contaminated,
> And you are innocent waters.

The music of "Quanto invidio" operates on the basis of a quasi-ostinato, a brief cadential pattern that repeats in the bass throughout the aria. This ostinato serves several functions, one of which is figurative: it represents aspects of the fountain that inspires Susanna's meditation. Obviously, music can represent water in many ways—this aria does not sound like Respighi, for instance, even if Stradella's experience with fountains was also Roman. What Stradella captures in his metaphor are qualities identified in the verbal text—clarity and innocence or purity—as well as a particular image of waves, in which similar units flow together to create an ongoing stream. Moreover, he exploits the "timeless" effect of ostinato procedures to invoke nature—a common association in seventeenth-century repertories.[20]

Stradella might have repeated the pattern unchanging as an orthodox ostinato. Instead, he modifies it so that it creates tensions both locally (as in the introduction, in which a polarity between tonic and dominant areas helps shape the phrase) and structurally (the aria pursues a sequence of modulations). He thereby produces a piece that exploits the image of obsession typical of the ostinato yet traces a dramatic trajectory of departure and return.

We might be tempted today to hear this modulatory schema either as stock formula or as a slightly primitive version of what soon establishes

Example 1.1: Stradella, *La Susanna*, "Quanto invidio"

itself as "purely musical." But given the structural flexibility of mid-seventeenth-century style, we can also hear it as a living procedure that kicks its way into existence for purposes of this piece in response to Stradella's needs of the moment. If something like this schema later freezes into "the way music goes," it is largely because of what the procedure is able to accomplish. But Stradella cobbles it together ad hoc from a number of the competing options available to him; his method more closely resembles bricolage than either formula or metaphysics.

We can sketch the assumptions of his practice relatively quickly. Stradella's task is to set a text as effectively as possible, both enhancing it affectively and articulating it structurally. Like most Western musicians, he accepts responsibility for ending in the same pitch area with which he began; he thus reinscribes the sense of centeredness that has been with us at least since the Franks imposed writing on Roman liturgical chant. But like other seventeenth-century Italian musicians, he also engages with various ways of expanding the peculiar capacities of cadential mechanisms.

As it had developed in the context of Renaissance polyphonic practice, the V-I harmonic cadence—hackneyed convention though it was—served as a mechanism to produce desires and fulfill expectations, and it did so more effectively than any other configuration available (Ex. 1.2a). Yet during the 1500s, the desires of the leading-tone harmony were usually short-lived: closure followed fast upon the heels of arousal, and another image emerged to accommodate the next line of lyrics. This process worked especially well for setting texts that delighted in sustained ambiguity and paradox: cinquecento compositions thrived on the style's relative looseness of syntax, which required clarification only at moments of musical punctuation. But for the late sixteenth-century composers who sought to appropriate some of the dramatic power generated by theatrical spectacle, the delicate ambiguity so carefully cultivated within the mannerist madrigal came to seem a liability.[21]

The technological breakthrough for theatrical realism came with *stile recitativo*, in which a composer throws a simple cadential formula

Example 1.2a: Dominant-tonic harmonic closure

Major version

I - V - I

Minor version

i - V - i

Example 1.2b: Linear cadential formulas

Major version

3  2, 3  (4 - 3  ) 2  1

Minor version

5  4  3  2  1

Example 1.2c: Background progression with tonal expansion
(minor version only)

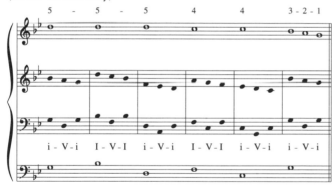

5 - 5 - 5  4  4  3 - 2 - 1

i - V - i  I - V - I  i - V - i  I - V - I  i - V - i  i - V - i

into the background and exploits its teleological force in shaping whole speeches (Ex. 1.2b). In order for the drive toward cadential closure to operate in an expanded state, the ear has to be led to hear as virtually causal the interconnections between successive moments of the formula. The innovations of the seventeenth century largely involve ways of harnessing the energy of that background syntax to produce longer and longer spans. Those surface harmonies we recognize as "tonal" (which are themselves nothing more than little cadence patterns) serve to sustain each moment in the background progression while simultaneously pointing toward—and thus producing desire for—its closure (Ex. 1.2c).

The whole procedure is posited on an uneasy, breathtakingly dynamic paradox: how to prolong a function through a process that can only keep going by means of patterns that constantly announce their impending termination. By 1700, these innovations will have stabilized sufficiently to grant the illusion of reason and order. In "Quanto invidio," however, the dependence of the measure-to-measure surface on the desire mechanism of the cadence remains palpable, for each unit of the ostinato figure performs a brief cadential pattern; each raises the expectation of imminent conclusion, and the impression of continuity that occurs results from the composer's ingenuity. If we leave the surface and take an overview of the background, we find a modulatory schema holding the aria together (I-V-vi-IV-V-I), which derives its cohesive power in large part from its own cadential origin, even though each point along the way is greatly prolonged.

Yet Stradella designs some aspects of the aria—even its structural pillars—not merely to produce the illusion of coherence but also to enhance affectively the sequence of thoughts presented in the libretto, as the words move from calm to abjection to exaltation. Moreover, in 1681 (before stabilized spans of a single key area become the norm) much of the music's delight involves the process of pushing further and further apart those pillars that constitute the background. Because the meaning of the words still informs much of the aria's unfolding— both the particular points of modulation and the degree of expansion given to each—we can fruitfully explain many of its musical events in terms of the verbal text. In other words, Stradella occupies a moment when the technologies of tonal expansion allow for extensive elaboration, yet his work predates the agendas of formal standardization brought about by composers such as Alessandro Scarlatti and Arcangelo Corelli: his pieces appear to make themselves up as they go, and although he wrote some pieces in ABA form, his arias typically arrange themselves as through-composed ABB' structures. The da capo convention, which comes to govern eighteenth-century opera as a formal fact of nature, shows up in Stradella's work as only one of many strategic alternatives.[22]

As is frequently the case in seventeenth-century arias, Stradella sets the initial lines of the lyrics in a relatively perfunctory manner: they serve principally to announce verbally the reigning trope. Thus he presents each of the first two lines in "Quanto invidio" once only. In the first, Susanna strives to conform to the cadential character of the ostinato, and it is only through additive means—that is, repeating her cadence—that she sustains the opening tonic as long as she does. Stradella marks the second line by moving directly into the dominant, where a vocal melisma imitates the water's flow. What will turn out to be the raison d'être of the aria—Susanna's successful emulation of the spring through the binding together of ostinato units—occurs first in measure 15, as a suspended E hovers over what would otherwise be a clear caesura, defying the gravitational pull toward immediate cadence.

The remaining two-thirds of the aria involves only the last two lines. Susanna's initial confession of contamination (m. 17) coincides metrically with the ostinato, yet her confession seems to corrupt the stream itself, as the whole piece pivots abjectly into B minor. Suddenly, in measure 26, the ostinato shifts to G, then back to tonic, where the focus shifts once again to the innocence of the waters. Formally the aria could end with its arrival on D, for it has accomplished syntactically what it had to do: that is, return to the original key. Instead, the voice embarks on an extraordinary melismatic expansion that in measure 42 even wrenches the ostinato from its regular course into a series of resisted cadences, enhancing the climactic illusion of infinitely swelling waters. In terms of the lyrics, Susanna's abjection turns into elation as she contemplates ideal purity; her initial reticence melts into ongoing ecstasy. This is Stradella's showcase moment: the passage where he gets to demonstrate his many ways of sustaining desire while delaying closure as long as possible.

In addition to demonstrating technical prowess and enhancing dramatic characterization, however, Stradella accomplishes other kinds of cultural work within the aria. As a soliloquy overheard, it grants the listener access to what is presented as Susanna's interiority. And while the lyrics themselves offer only a static comparison between her condition and the spring, the music sets them in such a way as to trace a succession of states, from calm, to alienation, to a confidence that simultaneously reestablishes security and launches a dynamic expansion of quite excessive length. We seem to witness her innermost doubts and her resolution of them within the music.

The fact that this shape (departing from tonal certainty and coming back) was becoming standardized at this time in no way diminishes our ability to hear it as Susanna's own personal drama: on the contrary, her emotional adventure makes sense to us precisely *because* it follows this shape. Indeed, it would be intelligible to us even without words—as it is in the sonatas of Corelli, one of the violinists in Stradella's pick-up orchestra. For this shape becomes not only "the way music goes" but also the way interior feelings—hers and ours—operate: it developed in the 1600s as one of the principal technologies for representing individualistic but "autonomous" subjectivities. If we now hear this convention as transcending culture, it is because the process has been replayed so often that it has been naturalized. Yet in "Quanto invidio," it is never entirely clear where tonality is operating as part of the expressive apparatus and where it serves the structural background. The two are virtually indistinguishable.

Unlike the only slightly later da capo arias, which carefully seal up any energy that might have been unleashed by such processes, "Quanto invidio" constantly threatens to spill over past its borders. To be sure, it is designed to do so, since it is but the first of three arias in a scena. But even the third aria of the set concludes not with its opening ritornello but rather with the ecstatic strain generated in its final section. The progressive dynamic of tonality as it emerged in the seventeenth century is very audible here; it will be the task of the eighteenth century to retain tonality's desire-producing capacity and yet contain far more securely this process that seeks by definition to overflow its boundaries. If some of the formal conventions of the 1700s seem quite uncompromising, it is in part because they were designed to cope with the overwhelming momentum generated through tonal trajectories. Yet regardless of how cleaned up tonality becomes, this unruly potential is always still sedimented in, always threatening to break out: seventeenth-century tonality is the skeleton in the closet, the capricious turtle beneath what we like to perceive as bedrock.[23]

*La Susanna* also participates in several other areas of cultural representation, including one quite alien to us now: namely, the sacred erotic. To many of us today, religion and sexuality reside at opposite ends of the spectrum. But seventeenth-century artists often mapped these realms upon one another because of many factors—including the charismatic example of St. Teresa, the increasing emphasis on subjective spirituality following the Reformation, and the need of the Counter Reformation church to attract and retain followers. If human desire is at its most fervent at moments of sexual transport, then the church wanted access to that experience, albeit harnessed and redefined as love for God.[24]

Like Claudio Monteverdi, Alessandro Grandi, Girolamo Frescobaldi, and Heinrich Schütz before him, Stradella here exploits this powerful cultural trope: Susanna's prolonged melisma constitutes a moment of transcendence, at once sacred and profoundly erotic. To quote St. Teresa, "The pain was so severe that it made me utter several moans. The sweetness caused by this intense pain is so extreme that one cannot possibly wish it to cease, nor is one's soul then content with anything but God. This is not a physical, but a spiritual pain, though the body has some share in it—even a considerable share. So gentle is the wooing which takes place between God and the soul that if anyone thinks I am lying, I pray God, in His goodness, to grant him some experience of it."[25]

Stradella here tries to replicate in music the effect of St. Teresa's prose descriptions or the sense of ecstasy captured by Bernini in his celebrated sculpture. Knowledge of this world—now mostly vanished— is necessary if we are to understand why the composer created that particular image at the end of "Quanto invidio": the task required his skills in harmonic manipulation, but the images he produced contributed to a very particular cultural preoccupation. Stradella hones his expansion devices—the very basis of later tonality—precisely to create such effects. Tonality emerges, in other words, as a mode of cultural representation, an instrument for the articulation and production of social values.[26]

Stradella's powerful depiction of Susanna is not without its ambivalences, however. If Renaissance paintings of Susanna often depicted her as an exhibitionist vainly contemplating herself in a mirror, Stradella's aria has Susanna display herself extravagantly: she flaunts the extremes of her vocal range, teases the listener's expectations, and finally delivers a prolonged, wordless climax. The elders soon accuse her of seducing them, and the testo's taunting commentary later in the oratorio likewise holds her responsible for her fate. Even Susanna admits her guilt eventually, as she confesses that her beauty itself caused her downfall and that of the elders. Of course, we do not actually *see* Stradella's Susanna in her bath; the medium of the oratorio demands that her irresistible sensuality be conveyed strictly by means of the ear. But the tonal devices that fuel her aria are too effective in their ability to arouse, too difficult to control once unleashed: she ought to have known better.

My point is not to castigate Stradella for sexist imagery but rather to draw attention to the cultural tensions revealed in this dramatization of the Susanna story, which pits the desire to indulge in intense sensuality against the need to frame and distance that sensuality—in part by projecting it onto a woman in a context that verbally condemns her for it. Mid-seventeenth-century composers came to specialize in depictions of the femme fatale (Poppea, Salome, Semiramide).[27] Such depictions not only acknowledge female sexuality but treat it with a blend of awe and fear—as do representations of St. Teresa or settings of the woman's verses from the Song of Songs.[28] For a variety of reasons, Baroque artists were obsessed with how to capture (in both senses of the word) the experience of feminine eroticism in their work, and this obsession left its marks both on the compositional techniques developed under its sway and on the bodies of male singers who sacrificed their all for the ability to simulate the sound of high-voiced ecstasy.

This set of representational practices stands in sharp contrast to those of later eras, several of which denied that women had sexual feelings at all. The Enlightenment sought to banish virtuosic women from the stage, thereby minimizing traces of female erotic transport (Mozart's Queen of the Night may be heard as a distant echo). And when the eighteenth century domesticated representations of women, it also—and not coincidentally—curbed the excesses of early tonality through increasing standardization (that melisma at the end of Susanna's aria would seem much safer if it were followed by a reassuring return to the beginning).[29] Thus although the narrative frame Stradella gives Susanna may be somewhat problematic, we can find in "Quanto invidio" a residue of the seventeenth-century belief that women experience both bodily and spiritual realms with unmatched intensity. If Susanna envies the fountain, Stradella envies her.

My second example also happens to belong to the category of the sacred erotic, though it comes from an unrelated practice that is vital and influential today: namely the gospel music of the African American church. The ensemble responsible for this tune, the Swan Silvertones, was formed in the early 1940s by Claude Jeter—coal miner, preacher, and incomparable falsettist—and they soon had a weekly radio show in Knoxville, sponsored by the Swan Bakery Company, from which they took their name.[30] In 1945 they began to record; by 1948 they were able to leave the coal mines behind and tour full time as professional musicians.[31] Membership in the group shifted periodically through the years (Jeter himself quit to concentrate on his ministry in 1963), but during their prime in the 1950s and early 1960s, they were among the most celebrated groups of their kind.

The Swan Silvertones recorded their performance of "Near the Cross" in 1959.[32] Since it is based on a traditional fundamentalist hymn, the full impact of the performance depends on the listener's having internalized the hymn itself, just as Bach expected his congregation to know by heart the chorales from which he constructed his preludes (Ex. 1.3). "Near the Cross" resembles many other such hymns: a verse of two phrases identical except for the cadences, respectively on dominant and tonic, and a chorus made up of a contrasting phrase and a return to the music of the second half of the verse. And although the hymn's composer, W. H. Doane, has thrown in a few of what my hometown congregation used to call "fancy" harmonies (vi in m. 2; a secondary dominant in the chorus on "raptured"), the principal moves in the hymn are supported with the most fundamental chords (tonic, dominant, subdominant), thereby producing the desired aura of inevitability and utter security.

African Americans first encountered hymns like "Near the Cross" in the massive evangelical movements that swept through the South in the nineteenth century. Whatever the motivation of those movements, the fervor of the fundamentalist message and its songs soon took root and developed within the slave population into a vibrant hybrid that blended elements of European music with practices handed down from African culture. After Emancipation, and especially after the breakdown of civil rights movements in the 1870s, the black church became the center of activity, the place where the community could maintain its identity and fight for survival—spiritual, social, and physical.[33]

Music holds a place of privilege in most African and African-based cultures, and it differs in many crucial respects from the European tradition. First, music is defined as an activity—something that exists only in as much as the community is involved in making it happen. It is far

Example 1.3: "Jesus, Keep Me Near the Cross"

**283**    **Jesus, Keep Me Near the Cross**

Fanny J. Crosby                                                    W. H. Doane

1. Je - sus, keep me near the cross: There a pre-cious foun-tain, Free to all, a
2. Near the cross, a trem-bling soul, Love and mer-cy found me; There the Bright and
3. Near the cross! O Lamb of God, Bring its scenes be-fore me; Help me walk from

healing stream, Flows from Calv'ry's mountain.
Morn-ing Star Sheds its beams a-round me.      In the cross, in the cross, Be my
day   to   day With its shad-ow o'er me.

glo - ry ev - er, Till my rap-tured soul shall find Rest be-yond the riv - er.

more oriented toward performance than producing objects, and performances are understood as the means whereby the community enacts
consolidation.[34] Second, while some individuals specialize in virtuosic
performance, all members of the society participate in the making of
music: it is a communal expression—as the hymn says, "free to all, a
healing stream." Accordingly, many African and African American
genres are characterized by the convention of call and response, in
which soloists are legitimated by the sonic embrace of the group.

Third, while individual improvisation is much treasured, it occurs within the context of frameworks passed on lovingly through the years. Henry Louis Gates Jr. has theorized this practice as "signifyin(g)," whereby the creative artist exhibits prowess and imagination and yet simultaneously reinscribes the cultural habits and structures that preserve both community and communication.[35] "Signifyin(g)" takes on many shapes, from the troping of familiar songs or stories to the use of a wide range of funky or "masked" sounds that incorporate elements of noise (deliberately exploiting complex vocal sounds, playing guitar with a bottleneck, and so on). But the polarization between self and society that led to the rejection of convention in European Romanticism would appear counterproductive within this diasporic community.[36]

Finally, many African musical practices insist on the strong presence of the body, even when it engages with religious beliefs. In traditional West African religions, a sign of a ritual's success is the entry of one or more participants into trance-state, where spirits inhabit temporarily the receptive believer's body. Music helps to break down barriers between members, to align soul and body, to facilitate spiritual transcendence—or "getting over," to use a familiar gospel expression.[37] And in virtually every African American genre from spirituals to rap, rhythmic pulsation serves to bring into being something of this sort of community.[38] This set of values made it possible for this group of forcibly displaced people to survive and maintain some sense of dignity despite the brutal conditions to which they were subjected. Music was and is still, for the most part, far too important for what Gregory Sandow once termed the "upward trivialization" of aesthetics.

One of the most striking aspects of the recording of Swan Silvertones performing "Near the Cross" is the model of social interaction to which it bears witness. Jeter, who sings lead vocals, performs his high-wire act safely supported not only by the steady regularity of the backup ensemble but also by an audience that responds enthusiastically to each of his virtuosic moves, encouraging him on to greater and greater heights. Jeter says concerning his artistic development: "So, I began making little falsetto notes and I noticed how people would like it. I began to rehearse it and do a little more. Then it got stronger and stronger and stronger."[39] In Stradella's "Quanto invidio," the illusion that we have direct access to Susanna's interiority requires the apparent absence of spectators (even if we are ever mindful of the elders lurking nearby in the bushes). But Jeter's virtuosity depends upon his audible, multileveled support system. He sings not just for himself but for his listeners, who perceive him as one who testifies for them all. The social context of performance is not only relevant here but indispensable. This recording permits us to hear the ritual enactment of that community as though firsthand.

As is typical, the backup singers provide the continuity for this performance. They sing in close harmony with velvety, well-rehearsed voices (characteristic also of contemporaneous doo-wop), enunciating text and inflecting pitches with great precision. The group credits their precision and sweetness of tone to their microphone skills, which they worked to perfect during their broadcast years. That is, the same amplification devices that made possible the intimate crooning of Bing Crosby also enabled the sounds cultivated by these new gospel ensembles. They even influenced Jeter's style of singing. As he says, "I believe in the soft approach. The Bible tells us, 'If you pray in secret, I'll reward you openly.' I tried to practice that during my career."[40] That "soft approach"—the apparent intimacy of Jeter's delivery—could not occur without the mediation of miking technologies.

When the backup singers enter, they lay down a slow groove that rocks the hymn physically. The groove registers even more powerfully in the chorus when clapping enters to mark the backbeats. As St. Teresa wrote of her ecstatic states, "the body has some part, even a considerable part, in it"; and even if we can't see the group moving with the pulse they create, we can hear their physical investment in the performance. To appreciate their performance properly—that is, to become part of the community here offered—we would have to surrender ourselves likewise to the groove, with all its carefully placed cross-rhythms.

The Silvertones have restructured the original hymn somewhat, throwing into stark relief the principal harmonic event of each line by singing the words on the tonic, then repeating them on the contrasting harmony—on the dominant- or subdominant-seventh, as the case may be. Instead of inflecting Fanny Crosby's poetry, as in the hymn, the chord changes here resemble a blues-like ritual, where the gravitational alternations among these basic tonal harmonies serve to mark our location within the framework.

While those chords carry something of their standard implications, the Silvertones deploy them in such a way as to attenuate the teleological drive with which they are usually associated in European music. Whereas the hymn dutifully works through to a restful tonic twice (at the end of verse and the end of chorus), the Silvertones defer closure in both places, postponing certainty with a suave diminished chord. The significance of this alteration becomes clear when the last line becomes the basis for sustained improvisation. As the backup group sings "just beyond the river" fifteen times, Jeter enacts his yearning to push through to another state of consciousness: he may be denied repose here on earth (or so the diminished chord at the end of each cycle indicates), yet he strives to get over, and he attains rapture through his efforts.

In some important sense, his performance is no simulation but an act of faith, and it is received as such by those listeners who respond so urgently to him. Jeter explains: "This is a thing where you can only survive by being real. Out of all the people we can fool, we can't fool God. He knows our intentions. So I'd rather fool nobody in the gospel field. If I don't feel the spirit, I won't move."[41] The recording concludes with a fade-out, but there is no reason why this cycling might not have lasted far longer—as long, in fact, as the energetic exchanges between the lead and congregation continued to inspire each other on to ever greater heights.

Jeter's reputation as a charismatic gospel singer rests on his ability to utilize effectively a wide range of rhetorical devices—that is, in his talent for "signifyin(g)." Nothing he does in this performance is exactly *new* (although his eerie falsetto moans are unmistakably his own),[42] but he brings these parts of a shared repertory together in a particularly compelling fashion. Musicologists might call some of his tactics "troping": that is, inserting connectives, editorial comments, and exclamations along the way, the way a preacher might in the heat of the sermon. What begins as a standard hymn becomes a personalized meditation, as Jeter throws in references to his family ("Mother told me that the fountain was free"), to his shortcomings ("Sometime I have to give up the right for the wrong down here"), and to his longing ("Come on Jesus, I need you and I can't get along without you this evening"). He thereby not only signifies, but he confesses his faith, failings, and hopes to the congregation. That his testimonial resonates with the larger group is evident by their echoes, cries of pleasure, and shouts of recognition.

Rhythmically, his tropes play off against the groove set out by the group. Sometimes he is relatively spare, adding brief statements only to bridge over the gaps between cycles; at other times, he throws in comments in such fevered succession that they threaten to overwhelm the groove: for instance, over line 3 he inserts "[Son, it don't cost you nothin', free to all a healin' . . . , all you got to do is believe on him, she said it] FLOWS." Both strategies demonstrate his rhythmic prowess: his ability to reinscribe the background by creating tensions against it, making it seem all the more inevitable when it enfolds him again.

Jeter's melodic fragments have little to do with the original tune. Once again, he is troping—playing around the borders and in the gaps of a well-known, much-loved hymn. His additions typically center on pitches most open to microtonal inflections and therefore affective intensity: the yearning sixth degree with which he begins his opening melisma on "Jesus"; the blue third degree that is bent down, in part to accommodate the frequent harmonic moves to $IV^7$, as on "Father, will you *keep* me"; or the raised fourth degree, used as an almost unbearable appoggiatura several times in the last section. Each of these is greeted enthusiastically by the audience, often inspiring Jeter to repeat that tactic or go it one better.

And, of course, Jeter draws on a large range of vocal sounds that seem to move beyond mere singing and into the phenomenology of spirit possession. The first of these occurs in the second line, on the first syllable of "fountain," and once more the audience voices its approval of this strange, disembodied sound. He marks the beginning of almost every line with a leap up to the high tonic pitch: if a kind of struggle is enacted in each cycle, that pure harmonic (which seems to pop out of nowhere) regularly restores our faith that we can, in fact, get over. Later, in the extended ostinato conclusion, he produces strangulated sounds and growls that mark a kind of limit to human expression.[43] As another singer (probably Louis Johnson) joins him in this final section, Jeter inserts ever more extreme devices into the gaps of that infinitely repeating riff, pushing himself and his listeners on to ecstasy. For the duration of the performance, we inhabit a world in which everyone participates, in which tradition balances with individual invention, in which self conjoins harmoniously with community, in which body, mind, and spirit collaborate, in which the possibility of a sustained present replaces tonality's tendency to strain for and against closure.

To be sure, African American music relies heavily on conventions—conventions that carry sedimented within them a worldview that has proved to be both durable and flexible. Indeed, it is in part the adaptability of African cultural attitudes—a willingness to fuse—that has ensured their survival. Not only do the Silvertones draw on the European-style hymn and African-based modes of performance in "Near the Cross," but they also gladly make use of the capacities of devices borrowed from pop genres (blues and crooning), modern sound technology (microphones and amplifiers), and the commercial networks afforded by radio, commercial promoters, and the recording industry.[44] And while they express their awareness of potential exploitation, they see commercial distribution as a way of getting the word out to an even larger community—and a way out of the crushing conditions of coal mining.

But no less does European music inscribe a world through its conventions and foundational assumptions. The society Stradella's music helped to shape was one that believed in unbridled progress and self-expression, that craved dramatic extravagance, that sought representations of interiority, that understood desire as the motivating element behind religion, sexuality, and musical procedures. It was a world that prized passion, eros, and spirituality. By sheer coincidence (that is, not because of mutual reliance on a shared convention), it shared more similarities with African American musical priorities than any European art repertory since: recall the quasi-improvisatory spontaneity, the drive for ecstasy, the emphasis on performativity rather than structural balance in Susanna's aria.

As we will see later, eighteenth-century musicians drew from the devices developed by composers such as Stradella what they found useful and thereby sustained a period of remarkable consensus in European music based on standardized tonal syntax and symmetrical forms. But before examining the practices that begin to prevail as "purely musical" during the Enlightenment, I will turn in the next chapter to the blues—a genre with tightly constrained formal parameters that has, nevertheless, given rise to much of the music that has shaped twentieth-century sensibilities.

The decentered approach to music history that will emerge over the course of this book differs considerably from the ones now generally circulating, which tend to take one repertory or another and create a narrative of origins and linear development. Without question, other historians would choose other elements—elements that would, of course, reflect their sense of the present as well as the kind of future they envision. But the existence of diverse historical narratives does not mean that such choices are either arbitrary or inconsequential. The recent canon wars revolve around which or whose turtles get to count in official records of cultural representation and reproduction. And a great deal is at stake in these debates, whether one claims on the one hand that a single tradition is to be maintained in the face of pluralism or, on the other, that such an account is no longer credible.

I should identify myself at this point as one who grew up listening to and playing virtually nothing but classical music. If I can be said to have a vernacular, Western classical music would have to be it. Yet I can no longer tell the stories about music I was trained to tell, for those stories marginalize or even exclude many of the musics that have been most influential—in the West and elsewhere—for the past hundred years.

I sometimes think that we musicologists resemble those pedagogues at the end of the seventeenth century who continued to advocate the *prima-prattica* style of Palestrina, who failed to notice that their world had come to be dominated by opera and its musical languages. Like them, we too often take our "purely musical" procedures to be absolute and use them in evaluating musics that work on the basis of radically different premises. I prefer to take as my model the great medieval theorist Grocheo, who impatiently pushed the "purely musical" speculations of Boethius to the side in order to produce a socially grounded inventory of the many distinct music cultures flourishing in Paris around 1300—an inventory that included explanations of the preferences of the aristocratic and ecclesiastical élites, the laboring classes, and even hot-blooded youths.[45] What would our histories look like if we took note of the many kinds of music surrounding us—observing differences in social function and technique, to be sure, but acknowledging them all nonetheless as parts of a shared universe?

My history of Western music contains Bach, Mozart, and Beethoven, but it also includes Stradella and the Swan Silvertones, Bessie Smith and Eric Clapton, k.d. lang, Philip Glass, and Public Enemy. And it treats all of them as artists who have negotiated with available conventions and in particular historical circumstances to produce musical artifacts of exceptional power and cultural resonance. If I can no longer privilege any one tradition, I find myself perpetually in awe of the countless ways societies have devised for articulating their most basic beliefs through the medium of sound; I share with philosopher Lydia Goehr the "sense of wonder at how human practices come to be, succeed in being, and continue to be regulated by one set of ideals rather than another."[46] Just turtles, perhaps. But what magnificent turtles!

CHAPTER 2

# Thinking Blues

One of the anxieties often voiced in accounts of twentieth-century music involves a construct called "the main stream." Donald Tovey's classic essay introduced the term to naturalize what we now refer to as "the canon," and many a composer and critic has attempted to trace the continuation of that main stream in the aftermath of World War I.[1] But as early as 1967, Leonard B. Meyer announced the futility of this venture, arguing instead that our time is characterized most by its stylistic pluralism.[2] Still, in narrative histories of twentieth-century music (by which is meant the continuation of Tovey's classical canon), musicologists continue to grope for the main stream, to grasp hopefully at various trickles, to lament the loss of orientation its disappearance has effected.

But if twentieth-century music has no single main stream, it does at least have something more coherent to bequeath the future than the various trickles we grasp at with a mixture of hope and despair. If I hesitate to label it *the* main stream, I have no qualms comparing it to a mighty river. It follows a channel cut by a force known as the blues.

We can trace something called blues back as far as the beginning of the twentieth century, and it has remained an active generator of new musical movements up until the present moment. When LeRoi Jones published his powerful book *Blues People* in 1963, his title referred to the African American musicians who fashioned the blues out of their particular historical conditions and experiences.[3] Yet a music scholar of a future time might well look back on the musical landscape of the 1900s and label us all "blues people": those who inhabited a period dominated by blues and its countless progeny.

That musical landscape would include such diverse items as the spiritual songs of Blind Willie Johnson, his proto-heavy-metal disciples Led Zeppelin, the stride piano of James P. Johnson, the earthy frankness of Ma Rainey and her heiress Janis Joplin, the electrified Chicago sound of Muddy Waters, the mournful country whine of Hank Williams, the exuberant Cajun stomp of Queen Ida and her Bontemps Zydeco Band, the elegant jazz arrangements of Duke Ellington, the gospel-tinged shouts of Little Richard as he ignited rock and roll, the adolescent surfer songs of the Beach Boys, James Brown's godfathering of soul, echoes from Nigerian and Zulu pop, the modernist irony of Thelonious Monk, the tormented quest for mystical union in albums by P. J. Harvey, the postmodern collages of John Zorn, not to mention contemporary resonances in rap. As much as these musics may differ from each other, they unite in engaging with the conventions of the blues.

Contrary to a popular belief that regards blues as some kind of unmediated expression of woe, the conventions underlying the blues secure it firmly within the realm of culture; a musician must have internalized its procedures in order to participate creatively within its ongoing conversation. Albert Murray writes:

> It is not a matter of having the blues and giving direct personal release to the raw emotion brought on by suffering. It is a matter of mastering the elements of craft required by the idiom. It is a matter of idiomatic orientation and the refinement of auditory sensibility in terms of idiomatic nuance. It is a far greater matter of convention, and hence tradition, than of impulse. . . . It is not so much what blues musicians bring out of themselves on the spur of the moment as what they do with existing conventions.[4]

And yet reliance on convention is rarely held to be incompatible with creativity in blues-based music. How does this musical universe operate, and what can we learn from it?

Before proceeding further, let me say a few words about my purpose in this chapter. I am not presuming to add anything substantial to available knowledge about blues: few genres of twentieth-century music have generated a more extended bibliography.[5] Likewise, I am not attempting to legitimate blues—this music and its practitioners do not need my help or the acknowledgment of academic musicology. Nor—let me hasten to assure you—am I setting up a comparison between African American and European-based musics in order to trash the latter. I promise to be just as affirmative in the next chapter on eighteenth-century tonal procedures.

I have two principal reasons for spending a chapter on this genre. First, I think that blues can help academic music study out of a long-standing methodological impasse: I am drawing on blues as a clear example of a genre that succeeds magnificently in balancing convention and expression, and I will make use of this model as I reexamine the European eighteenth century in chapter 3. Second, I firmly believe that any account of twentieth-century Western music must dwell extensively on the blues in its various manifestations because this is the music that has most shaped our era. Finally, the blues-based repertory deserves our careful attention simply because it contains so much superb music, and I take this to be among the principal reasons we bother to study any repertory.

The blues is largely the product of a diasporic people, though the genre did not originate in Africa. When procedures recognizable as blues first entered the historical record around 1900, they already testified to centuries of fusions with North American genres. I have occasionally heard the claim that no trace of Africa remains in the blues, that African practices were thoroughly eradicated from the music of black people under slavery, and that we must admit this, even while we may mourn the loss involved.[6] And without question, blues harmonies bear witness to European influence—the result of exposure to hymns, dances, popular ballads, fiddle tunes, and marches that circulated widely in the United States during the nineteenth century. Most of the instruments played by blues musicians originated in Europe; lyrics are sung in English; and, as Jones and Lawrence Levine have pointed out, even the emphasis on individual subjectivity in blues poetry and music resembles European practices more than those of Africa.[7]

But most specialists—including not only Jones and Levine but also (among many others) Gunther Schuller, Olly Wilson, Christopher Small, Henry Louis Gates, Peter van der Merwe, Paul Gilroy, and Samuel Floyd—identify in the blues a great many typically African elements.[8] They argue persuasively that African Americans—long after having been uprooted from their homelands and against enormous odds—managed to maintain and transmit a core of collective memory while in exile, especially through their music. For example, blues musicians privilege a vast palette of sounds that European-trained ears tend to hear as distorted or out of tune. As Ernest Borneman explained in a classic essay from the 1940s:

> While the whole European tradition strives for regularity—of pitch, of time, of timbre and of vibrato—the African tradition strives precisely for the negation of these elements. In language, the African tradition aims at circumlocution rather than at exact definition. The direct statement is considered crude and unimaginative; the veiling of all contents in ever-changing paraphrases is considered the criterion of intelligence and personality. In music, the same tendency towards obliquity and ellipsis is noticeable: no note is attacked straight; the voice or instrument always approaches it from above or below, plays around the implied pitch without ever remaining any length of time, and departs from it without ever having committed itself to a single meaning. The timbre is veiled and paraphrased by constantly changing vibrato, tremolo and overtone

effects. The timing and accentuation, finally, are not *stated*, but *implied* or *suggested*. The musician challenges himself to find and hold his orientation while denying or withholding all signposts.[9]

The rhythmic patterns that animate any given realization of blues likewise are related to African attitudes and tied to a vocabulary of physical gestures, kinesthetic motions, and dance steps quite unlike anything European. Music in many African cultures is inseparable from dance on the one hand and spirituality on the other. Historian Sterling Stuckey writes: "For the African, dance was primarily devotional, like a prayer. . . . The whole body moving to complex rhythms . . . was often linked to the continuing cycle of life, to the divine."[10] Thus the groove that sustains the blues serves as a conduit linking the body, words, musicians, listeners, and a realm often experienced as sacred. As we saw in the gospel music of the Swan Silvertones in chapter 1, no transcendence without the body, no individual redemption without the community.

Most important is the way the blues operates according to certain models of social interaction characteristic of African cultures. The practice nineteenth-century blacks called signifying—long before Henry Louis Gates revived the word as "signifyin(g)" for fashionable critical jargon—strives to maintain a socially shared framework within which participants exhibit prowess and virtuosity through highly individualized elaborations. Signifyin(g) thus ensures the continuity of community, at the same time that it celebrates the imagination and skill of each particular practitioner. Gates developed his theory of signifyin(g) in order to account for why African American writers often prefer to reinhabit conventional structures rather than treat formal innovation as the be-all-and-end-all of literary value, as it is for many European-based artists and critics. And he drew heavily on the example of blues in explaining this alternative worldview that pervades so many African American cultural activities.

We cannot trace the precise history of the blues, for those who had the means of preserving music before the twentieth century did not often write down the music produced by African Americans. Occasionally a style ascribed to the black population sparked a response among European or Euro-American musicians, but we cannot tell much about the original music itself from these appropriations—except that its relation to the body and its affective qualities appealed to those with access to notation.[11]

The blues seems to have emerged from many different kinds of musics, including shouts, spirituals, gospel hymns, field hollers, ritual laments, dances, and virtually every musical genre that African Americans had encountered. Whatever its history as a strictly oral practice, we can trace the genre with confidence only after it entered into writing. The first "recording" of blues per se came from the pen of W. C. Handy in 1912, who was promptly granted the title "Father of the Blues."[12] But even as Handy was composing his blues, a far more powerful form of writing—sound recording—was making its first appearances, and it is to this technology that we owe most of what we know about blues history.

It is important to keep in mind that recording and its commercial distributing networks did not merely preserve this music; it also actively shaped the blues as we know it. We cannot, in any case, recover whatever it was that existed before notation and recording crystallized it into something like its standard format. Among the first commercial successes of the new medium were the recordings of the blues queens, Ma Rainey, Bessie Smith, Ida Cox—women who blended modes of performance borrowed from church, rural entertainments, vaudeville, and urban popular idioms when they sang songs such as Handy's "St. Louis Blues" and their own compositions. The Mississippi Delta bluesmen of the late 1920s and the 1930s, many of whom were discovered by recording agents scouring the South for material to supply the burgeoning market of black consumers, had been heavily influenced by early commercial recordings.[13] Even so "authentic" a musician as Robert Johnson learned in part from listening to Bessie Smith on 78s, and he tailored his own songs to accommodate the three-minute limit of sound-recording technology.

In other words, no matter how deeply we excavate the blues in search of a bedrock of pure folk music, we always find the mediating presence of the culture industry.[14] Yet, as George Lipsitz has argued with respect to popular culture and ethnic identity over the course of this century, uncovering commercial interventions in such a genealogy does not discredit it.[15] For it has not been despite but rather *by means of* the power of mass mediation that the explosive energies of the blues managed to spread and develop in as many directions as it did; even so influential an artist as Ma Rainey was unknown outside the South until Paramount Records signed her in 1923.[16] And while the threat of cooptation always accompanies the commercial media, so do the possibilities of worldwide distribution, dialogue across the barriers of class and race, and the unpredictable responses and tangents of development that can proceed from such heightened visibility and audibility.

We often underestimate the impact of the technology of writing on medieval music or of commercial printing on culture since the Renaissance, but it is much more difficult to ignore the cultural explosion made possible by twentieth-century innovations. With sound recording, a previously silenced group, which had been represented to the broader public (when at all) only through European notation, descriptions, and imitations, could begin to explore and literally to broadcast their own various approaches to self-representation. To be sure, these new voices had to negotiate with those who regulated the industry, and the abuses that resulted have sometimes seemed to outweigh the triumphs. Yet this chain of negotiations has had the effect of altering in an African direction the worldwide history of music, the body, sensibilities, and much else.

## TWELVE-BAR BLUES

Viewed from a European vantage point and with European criteria, the blues might seem impoverished. Indeed, a more rigid convention is difficult to imagine, as a three-phrase harmonic pattern with a two-line poetic scheme is repeated in verse after verse, blues number after blues number. And yet it is the formulaic status of that pattern that has enabled it to give rise to so many rich and varied repertoires, that allowed it to function so effectively as what literary critic Houston Baker calls a matrix of African American memory, to sustain personalized improvisation, to maximize communication and the immediate appreciation by listeners of even the most minute inflections.[17]

I have chosen one of the best-known blues—the opening verse of W. C. Handy's "St. Louis Blues," as performed by Bessie Smith and Louis Armstrong—to serve as a schematic model for the blues procedure.[18] For each line of lyrics, I have indicated the underlying harmony for each successive bar, along with common alternatives. Even when performed by a single musician (as in the example below by Robert Johnson), each four-bar section operates on the basis of a call/response mechanism, with two bars of call followed by two of instrumental "response."

| Line 1: | I hate to see | the ev'ning sun go | down | |
| (1–4 mm.) | I | IV (or I) | I | I⁷ (V of IV) |

| Line 2: | I hate to see | the ev'ning sun go | down | |
| (5–8) | IV | IV | I | I |

| Line 3: | It makes me think I'm | on my last go | round. | |
| (9–12) | V | IV (or V) | I | (V⁷) |

Unlike the harmonic practices of European classical music (which is where individualistic expression is most often registered), the changes in the standard twelve-bar blues serve as a dependable, little-changing background that articulates the formal divisions within the lyrics and heightens the rhetorical distinctions among the lines of text. Typically, the first phrase is harmonically static, beginning and ending as it does on the tonic, though it may be inflected to IV in bar 2. Following the two-bar "call" (the verbal statement), the "response" stays grounded on the tonic, though a seventh often enters in preparation for the move to IV.

The second phrase repeats the first line of text, but this time it begins on IV. The "call" takes place in this other harmonic region, then returns to I for a cadence at the beginning of bar 7; the "response" maintains this area of repose. To be sure, the alternation between these two closely related chords—I and IV—creates only a slight degree of tension. Yet it allows for two quite different interpretations of a single line of text: the stable "call" of the first line gets unsettled by its response, leading to a reconsideration of the "call" in the second line, cast now in the new light of a changed harmonic context. A blues singer will usually convey subtle but distinctly different implications of that line when she or he presents it a second time with the harmony tilted slightly askew. Moreover, the second "response" stabilizes by returning to the tonic rather than pushing toward reorientation as in the first line. Thus, even if these fundamental harmonies ensure maximal security, such minimal alterations permit a significant shift in tone. The result is something like the harmonic equivalent of a cross-rhythm, with textual sameness and harmonic sameness held in tension against one another.

The most dramatic contrast comes with the beginning of the third line, which delivers the consequent—the anticipated punchline—to the twice-stated first line of the lyrics. This moment is highlighted by a move to V, which usually relaxes after a bar to IV, and then returns back to I. Note that the harmonic rhythm gradually accelerates through the three segments of the blues: the first line sustains a single area for four bars, and the second spends two bars each on IV and I. Now the harmonies begin to shift every bar, producing greater animation, and placing a strong accent halfway through the "call." In fact, the "call" this time may move through three harmonies, V-IV-I, underscoring the sentiment expressed there; if the first line throws out a proposition, the second mulls over it, and the third draws emphatic conclusions.

Harmonic closure arrives punctually at the beginning of bar 11, yet musicians typically undermine that sense of an ending by stepping away from I to $V^7$, then building momentum through a "turnaround" that pushes forward into the next cycle. These junctures between verses count as among the most important musical challenges for performers, as they work to arouse a desire for continuation. A good blues band can keep going indefinitely—all night long, as they often boast— by converting what is technically an additive structure into an ever-changing process in which every detail "signifies." Like Scheherazade, blues performers learn how to imply certainty, then suspend it long enough to hook the listener into anticipating another round. And still another. If (unlike Scheherazade) their lives don't depend on the success of their strategies, their livelihoods do.[19]

This simple procedure turns out to be exceptionally resilient, capable of undergirding the most varied of subjects, affects, and styles. If individual blues chords do not operate on the basis of deviation for purposes of expression (as, for instance, an unexpected Neapolitan or a move to ♭VI might in a Schubert song), they do underwrite a powerful rhetorical structure, and the dynamic they chart has been refined by many generations of performers interacting with audiences. While our attention focuses on the imaginative nuances displayed by each new instantiation of the blues, the facilitating pattern itself counts as the most important signifier in the lot: it acknowledges a social history, a lineage descending from a host of tributaries. And with each verse, each performance, it reinscribes a particular model of social interaction.

Within the context of each particular manifestation, however, few people listening to the blues pay much attention to the pattern itself. If the pattern guarantees coherence and the survival of collective memory, it also hovers in the background, accommodating and articulating (as though "naturally") the project at hand. Thus in order to appreciate how the blues operates as a cultural force, we need to examine closely some specific moments and tunes.

It would be absurd to try to treat a genre as pervasive as blues comprehensively in such a short space. My purpose here is to try to demonstrate a critical approach that takes into account the conventions of blues and historical context, as well as the particularities of the music itself. Accordingly, I will confine myself in this chapter to addressing three tunes only, representing women's Classic Blues, Delta blues, and the blues-based rock of the late 1960s. I will return to the blues in the final chapter when I deal with contemporary compositions by John Zorn, Prince, and Public Enemy that engage once again with blues patterns—no longer as the conventional space they inhabit but as the locus of shared cultural memory, available for citation in the production of new meanings.

## BESSIE SMITH: "THINKING BLUES"

Bessie Smith was known during her illustrious career as the Empress of the Blues. Like many of the black women who became stars during the first decade of mass-mediated recording, Smith regarded blues as only one of several marketable genres. For although born and raised in Tennessee, she learned about blues not from oral tradition but from her mentor and rival Ma Rainey; Rainey in turn had learned this mode of expression—at least according to her testimony—from a young girl whom she overheard singing to herself after one of Rainey's tent shows, sometime during the first decade of the century. Rainey incorporated blues into her act (Ma and Pa Rainey, "Assassinators of the Blues," with the Rabbit Foot Minstrels) and found that her audiences responded enthusiastically when she offered them what they perceived as their own music. Smith absorbed both style and format, then, from a context devoted to public entertainment, and when she moved into more urban environments, she continued fusing blues with the popular songs of vaudeville and with a newly emerging idiom known as jazz.

As I have already mentioned, by the time blues started showing up in written or recorded form, it already had merged with commercial enterprises. Yet there exists a cultural mythology (stemming largely from the 1960s and for reasons we will explore later) that wants to trace a pure lineage of blues from a cluster of rural, male blues singers recorded in the 1930s. And that mythology tends either to erase the women who first brought the blues to broad public attention or else to condemn them for having compromised that pure lineage with commercial popular culture.

But Simon Frith and Howard Horne have suggested that the reason for this marginalization might involve even more complex cultural tensions. If the blues came to represent an unassailably virile form of masculinity to British rockers (the musicians largely responsible for the mythologizing of Delta blues), then women could not be acknowledged at all in the canon—let alone as its progenitors. Frith and Horne go on to explain that this association in England of blues/rock with manliness may help account for why so few women art-school students in the 1960s turned to music for self-expression; they became, instead, the vanguard of feminist visual and performance artists.[20] Although these are the concerns of a later and very different group of listeners/ practitioners, they have, in effect, shaped the ways we now usually understand the historical role and contributions of women blues singers.

Purity and authenticity were rarely urgent matters for working black musicians who had to negotiate with real conditions—the securing of gigs, audiences, recording deals—or else face destitution. And prevailing conditions differed considerably according to gender. Male bluesmen often took the option of roaming through the region, playing on the streets, in juke joints, or at festivities as opportunities arose. As a result, many of them remained closely tied to and sustained by the traditional community. Women did not have access to the same kind of mobility, and few became itinerant musicians. Yet with the increasing instability of the southern black population at the turn of the century— the massive migrations to northern cities motivated by poverty, Jim Crow laws, and lynchings—women, too, often were compelled to leave home. By and large, however, they sought the security of steady employment. As Daphne Harrison has shown, many of the performers who came to be celebrated as the blues queens were displaced young women who found they could patch together a living performing in traveling minstrel shows, vaudeville, urban clubs, and (after the industry reluctantly agreed to try black women singers) the new medium of recording.[21]

What resulted was an explosion of female creativity that animated the 1920s—one of the few such moments in Western music history. These women and the market they helped produce exerted significant cultural and economic power for about a decade. As *The Metronome* reported in January 1922 (a scant two years after Mamie Smith recorded the first blues number), "One of the phonograph companies made over four million dollars on the Blues. Now every phonograph company has a colored girl recording. Blues are here to stay."[22]

If the blues produced under these conditions bear traces of its social contexts, that makes it no different from any other kind of music. Rather than hearing women's jazz-and-pop-flavored blues as corrupt, writers such as Hazel Carby, Daphne Harrison, and Toni Morrison have treated it as a genre that registered with keen accuracy the shocks and jolts of early black urban life, including the first direct encounters of the black population with the pressures of capitalist economies.[23] If some of us prefer to turn to the rural bluesmen in an imagined pastoral setting, it is partly because we can thereby pretend to retreat from the harsh realities of industrialized modernity.

One of the extraordinary contributions of so-called Classic Blues is its articulation of desire and pleasure from the woman's point of view. Throughout the span of Western culture, women have been spoken for more than they have been permitted to speak. And given the tendency for women to be reduced to sexuality and the body, many female artists have tried to avoid this terrain altogether.[24] As a result, vocabularies of the body and of erotic feelings have been constructed principally by men, even when they are projected onto women, as in opera and much popular music. Thus the blues queens offer an unparalleled moment in the history of cultural representation. As Carby puts it:

What has been called the "Classic Blues" . . . is a discourse that
articulates a cultural and political struggle over sexual relations:
a struggle that is directed against the objectification of female
sexuality within a patriarchal order but which also tries to reclaim
women's bodies as the sexual and sensuous subjects of women's
song. . . . The women blues singers occupied a privileged space;
they had broken out of the boundaries of the home and taken their
sensuality and sexuality out of the private into the public sphere. [25]

Accounting for how and why this happened is very complex. On the
one hand, African-based cultures tend to treat the body and eroticism as
crucial elements of human life: the shame or prurience that attends sexuality in so many European cultures is often absent. But on the other hand,
the bodily components of African American culture have repeatedly been
misconstrued within the dominant society.[26] Because black women were
often defined as oversexed by whites,[27] it was risky for them to sing explicitly about desire: entrepreneurs in the culture industry cheerfully ex-
ploited the stereotype of the libidinal black female in posters, sheet music,
and staging (recall, for instance, the salacious marketing of so brilliant a
performer as Josephine Baker); and singers who lacked clout sometimes
were pressured into prostitution, which resided just next door to entertainment, as Billie Holiday's painful memoirs make clear. They also encountered severe castigation from the black middle class, which often
adopted the mores and attitudes of white bourgeois culture.

This was yet another set of issues that had to be negotiated with great
care by each female performer, within each song. Despite the personal
dangers and social controversies, however, these women left us an invaluable legacy revealing how female pleasure, sexual independence,
and woman-to-woman address could sound—a legacy Angela Davis
does not hesitate to identify as feminist.[28] Several of them, including
Rainey and Smith, even celebrated their bisexuality in their lyrics.

I want to focus now on "Thinking Blues," one of Bessie Smith's own
blues numbers, which was recorded in New York in 1928.[29] Smith's
lyrics in "Thinking Blues" deal with some of the central themes of

women's blues: broken relationships, remorse, and pleading. Yet in contrast to some of the male-composed lyrics she also performed superbly, "Thinking Blues" articulates a vision of female subjectivity that balances self-possessed dignity with flashes of humor and a powerfully embodied sense of the erotic; simply the stress on the verb "to think" in the opening and final lines presents a different kind of experience from the passive suffering often ascribed to women in general and Smith in particular.[30]

BESSIE SMITH: "THINKING BLUES"

Did you ever sit thinking with a thousand things on your mind?
Did you ever sit thinking with a thousand things on your mind?
Thinkin' about someone who has treated you so nice and kind.

Then you get an old letter and you begin to read,
You get an old letter and you begin to read,
Got the blues so bad, 'til that man of mine I wanna see.

Don't you hear me, baby, knockin' on your door?
Don't you hear me, baby, knockin' on your door?
Have you got the nerve to drive me from your door?

Have you got the nerve to say that you don't want me no more?
Have you got the nerve to say that you don't want me no more?
The Good Book says you got to reap what you sow.

Take me back, baby, try me one more time.
Take me back, baby, try me one more time.
That's the only way I can get these thinking blues off my mind.

*Bessie Smith, "Thinking Blues." Used by permission of Hal Leonard Corporation.*

As is the case in many blues numbers, "Thinking Blues" suggests a possible narrative framework but moves freely among many forms of implied address from verse to verse. Sometimes she hails the listener as though in conversation ("Did you ever sit thinking?"); at other times, she seems to retreat into soliloquy ("Then you get an old letter"); and finally, she speaks as though directly to the man whom she has evidently left and whom she wants back. As she approaches him, she moves from tentative questioning ("Don't you hear me knocking?"), to audacity ("Do you have the nerve to say?"), to demands ("Take me back, baby").

Thus while there is a clear rhetorical shape to the sequence of five choruses—a move from public address to internalized reflection to simulated encounter, a steady increase in intensity—the blues convention that underlies the piece minimizes the narrative component of the music itself. What we get instead is a series of meditations on a single situation, as Smith returns to the problem nagging her with a new approach in each verse. The repetitions suggest personal obsession, but at the same time, her use of the blues invites the listener to identify with her predicament. What she sings sounds utterly familiar: we can relate. As John Coltrane once said, the audience heard "we" even if the singer said "I."[31] She invokes and brings into being a temporary community that bears witness to and empathizes with her subjective expression, made intersubjective by her use of shared codes.

Yet as transparent as it may seem, her performance refuses to offer a single easily identified affect—even within any particular verse. The structure of the blues, in which the first line of each chorus occurs twice, permits her to shift her implications radically from moment to moment. She couches each statement within an apparently limitless range of ambiguities and ambivalences—she lives a gray area, never truly giving anything away even while suggesting a whole range of possibilities.

At times her moans seem to spell grief, but in the next moment a similar glissando will suddenly turn into a sly, insinuating grind. On "Have you got the nerve to say that you don't want me no more?" is she seducing? Groveling? Taunting? And taunting her lover or herself? This sentence is a central event in the song, and she turns it every which way but loose. Yet what is she saying underneath all those layers of irony? The final line, "Take me back, try me one more time," clarifies a great deal—this is what she wants; no more indirection. But while her words may plead, the power of her delivery and her nuances destabilize the potential abjection of her appeal. This lady is in charge, even if she "ain't too proud to beg."

In "Thinking Blues," the musicians elect the option of remaining on V for bars 9 and 10 rather than moving down through IV. We may never know who chose to do it this way, but the rhetorical effect is to maintain a single, steady affect through the last line until the moment of cadence in bar 11. Smith's delivery of each verse's final line takes advantage of this detail by driving all the way through rather than releasing the energy in stages, and it becomes especially insistent in verses 3 ("have you got the nerve to drive me from your door?") and 4 ("the Good Book says you got to reap what you sow").

In this recording, Smith is accompanied by some of her favorite sidemen: Demas Dean on cornet, Fred Longshaw on piano, the incomparable Charlie Green on trombone. All three were jazz musicians—Green played regularly with Fletcher Henderson—and the performance presents a fusion between the demands of jazz ensemble-playing and the more intimate qualities of the blues. One of the most obvious jazz elements is standardization: in order to facilitate group improvisation, the blues pattern here (and elsewhere in Classic Blues) has been regularized, so that each chorus follows the twelve-bar progression.

Consistent with the blues, however, is their style of bending pitches, rhythms, timbres, and rhetorical conventions to signify on the standard pattern. The song is structured according to call and response, with Dean and Green answering Smith in turn on alternate lines, thus playing up the asymmetries already inherent in the pattern. Each instrumentalist carefully links his contributions with Smith's words and expressive decisions: in other words, all elements of the song—whether sung or played—are vocal in conception and execution. Green and Dean never tire of intensifying or ironicizing Smith's inflections. Green tends to get down with her growls and innuendoes, while Dean contributes astringent, strutting countermotives that keep Smith and her trombonist from spiraling too deeply into the funky zone. Even

Langshaw—whose principal task it is to maintain the harmonies and the groove at the piano—throws in subtle melodic comments and echoes here and there.

Not only do Smith's three instrumentalists amplify the various shadings of her delivery (they act as extensions of her utterances), but they also serve as an exemplary cluster of listeners who react audibly to her calls, thus granting her the social legitimation of community. If technology had permitted a live performance, we would also hear actual listeners lending their support (as in the Swan Silvertones tune discussed in chapter 1) through sympathetic moans, appreciative hoots for the double entendres, and responses such as "Sing it, Bessie!" or (as we would put it today) "You go, girl!"

## ROBERT JOHNSON, "CROSS ROAD BLUES"

When the blues queens proved to be commercially viable, recording companies sent agents out in search of other talent that would appeal to the African American market now being aggressively cultivated. At the same time (the late 1920s and 1930s), folklorists such as Alan Lomax also began traveling through the South in hopes of recording and preserving musics that were in danger of disappearing with the massive migrations north and the onslaught of the mass media. What both commercial scouts and ethnomusicologists found were large numbers of itinerant musicians who performed for various occasions within black rural communities.

Unfortunately, the Great Depression brought to an end the boom that had carried Bessie Smith to fame, and recording companies grew reluctant to gamble on unknown genres or talents. Thus much of what was collected from rural bluesmen circulated only as "race" records designated exclusively for the African American market or as field recordings harvested for purposes of ethnographic study. In the late 1930s, John Hammond—an executive at Columbia Records and a blues aficionado—began to mount prestigious concerts of such musicians, along with jazz figures. Around that same time, musicians who had migrated to northern cities were developing urban versions of downhome music that would become extremely influential. Many later blues stars (e.g., Muddy Waters, B. B. King) learned their trade from those earlier musicians—often through recordings. But the bids for commercial success by the Delta bluesmen had occurred at precisely the wrong time.[32]

Robert Johnson figures foremost among this group. Held up as a legend by Waters and made into a virtual god by the British rockers who rediscovered him in the 1960s, he spent his short career playing gigs throughout the South, with side trips to Chicago and New York. In the mid-1930s, Johnson sought out a recording agent, who undertook two sessions with him: three days in November 1936, two in June 1937. In all, he cut eleven 78s, one of which ("Terraplane Blues") sold reasonably well within the southern race-record circuit. But by the time John Hammond tried to recruit him for his 1939 Carnegie Hall concert, Johnson was dead—apparently poisoned by a jealous husband.

Johnson's posthumous reputation rests on an LP released by Columbia in the 1960s. Executives at Columbia speculated that rock'n'roll had generated a market that might be receptive to rock's forerunners, and they turned to their archives for possible materials. Later in this chapter I will discuss some reasons why Johnson became an idol for musicians in England. But for now I want to examine one of his most celebrated cuts, "Cross Road Blues."[33]

ROBERT JOHNSON: "CROSS ROAD BLUES"
I went to the crossroad, fell down on my knees,
I went to the crossroad, fell down on my knees,
Asked the Lord above "Have mercy, save poor Bob if you please."

Standin' at the crossroad, I tried to flag a ride,
Standin' at the crossroad, I tried to flag a ride,
Didn't nobody seem to know me, everybody pass me by.

The sun goin' down, boy, dark gon' catch me here,
Oooo, boy, dark gon' catch me here,
I haven't got no lovin' sweet woman that love and feel my care.

You can run, you can run, tell my friend boy Willie Brown,
You can run, tell my friend boy Willie Brown,
Lord, that I'm standin' at the crossroad, babe, I believe I'm sinkin'
    down.

One of the first things that strikes the ear in "Cross Road" is the peculiar, almost throttled intensity of both guitar and vocal sounds. Although Johnson recorded several very erotic, seductive, slow-hand blues, his posthumous fame rests with these rather more tortured numbers. An affect of dread and entrapment pervades this tune—partly the result of his strangulated, falsetto vocals and his uncanny replication of that timbre on the guitar. Moreover, Johnson's percussive guitar pulse, which locks in at the eighth-note level, allows almost no sensual movement: even though Johnson's singing constantly strains against that beat, the listener's body is regulated by those short, aggressively articulated units. The guitar thus seems to represent simultaneously both oppressive outside forces and a desperate subjectivity fighting vainly for escape.

Another factor contributing to the effectiveness of "Cross Road Blues" is its elastic sense of phrasing. Because he performs by himself, Johnson has no need to follow the standardized organization of ensemble blues, whereby each line receives four bars. Instead, phrase-length becomes one more element he can manipulate rhetorically. Typically, in "Cross Road" Johnson lingers after the first line, as his call is met with a varying number of guitar riffs that seem to obstruct his progress. The presentation of the second line operates similarly, with erratic extensions. But the final phrase often sounds truncated, with some bars of three rather than four beats. And no sooner does he achieve the conventional closure of the culminating line than he plunges on, as though dissatisfied, back into the maelstrom. He grants little relief here—as though hesitation at the cadence would mean that the devil (to whom Johnson's peers believed he had sold his soul in exchange for his guitar technique) would claim him. This phrase irregularity, then, is not a sign of primitivism (he had listened to Classic Blues on the phonograph as much as anyone, and many of his other numbers adhere to the twelve-bar paradigm), but rather a parameter he bends as willfully as pitches, rhythms, and timbres: even the meter expands and contracts to accommodate his rhetorical impulse.

As idiosyncratic as "Cross Road" may be, it relies on the blues format both for its affective quality of obsession and for its public intelligibility. Indeed, Johnson takes for granted that his audience knows the harmonic framework within which he operates: the changes themselves are often only suggested as he concentrates instead on the pungent guitar riff that haunts the song.[34] No longer just a glorified accompaniment pattern or the expected response to fill in the time between vocal lines, the riff comes to dominate "Cross Road," serving double duty both as the amplification of the vocalist's affect and as the object of dread against which he strains. The cross-rhythms set up within the guitar seem to allow no airspaces, no means of escape. Unlike "Hellhound Blues," another of Johnson's songs of metaphysical entrapment, there are no moments of relief—no ribald references to making love while awaiting doom. Instead we are locked into two-and-a-half minutes of concentrated horror—intense social alienation, images handed down from African *vodun* (which holds the cross road to be the terrain of Legba), and the entirely justified fear of what might well befall a black man in Mississippi in the 1930s caught outside after sundown.

Since the 1960s, blues musicians such as Johnson have been elevated as the authentic wellspring from which parasitic, commercially contaminated genres drew their strength. Yet, as George Lipsitz has argued so eloquently, this dichotomy accomplishes little more than ideological mystification.[35] To be sure, Johnson's audience was predominantly composed of southern rural African Americans whose vernacular was blues. He never garnered the prestige to negotiate seriously with a broader, mixed public. Yet it seems quite certain that he happily would have done so, given the opportunity. He was very much a product of his moment in history: his music was influenced by what he had access to by means of recording and radio; he performed Tin Pan Alley songs at his gigs; he drew on the latest technologies (automobile engines, the phonograph) to create some of his most memorable tropes; he sought out recording agents himself. Had he lived, he would probably have moved north and participated in the transformation of traditional blues into R & B. To hold him as the authentic measure against which to condemn both his successors and female predecessors is to cling to a shredded mythology of Romanticism that ought to be laid to rest.

## CREAM, "CROSSROADS"

> White folks got money,
> Colored folks got all the signs.
> Signs won't buy nothin'. (1845)[36]

My third example requires that we jump from the rural South to the English art schools of the 1950s and early 1960s. For one of the most unlikely events in recent cultural history involves a group of disaffected art students (including Keith Richards, Pete Townsend, Freddy Mercury, Jimmy Page, Charlie Watts, Cat Stevens, and Eric Clapton; Mick Jagger was from the more upscale London School of Economics)[37] who embraced traditional blues as their own musical language and turned it into what became known in North America as "the British Invasion." Their motivation had at least as much to do with their own context as with the particular music they embraced to form their identities. Yet there are reasons why they chose blues rather than any of the other culturally distant musics available.

The bohemian subculture flourishing around art schools in the 1940s had adopted Dixieland jazz as a sign of proletarian sympathies and resistance to commercialism.[38] When bebop broke on the scene, English jazz aficionados split between those who advocated the "progressive" sounds of modern jazz and those who sought authenticity in "trad" (i.e., Dixieland). In the 1950s, the debate shifted ground somewhat, as John Mayall started to push the blues as an even more authentic source than jazz. Many younger students, who wanted to mark their distinction from the earlier generation, followed Mayall and re-created much the same debate, but now with blues representing authenticity against the commercialism of jazz *tout court*. (This may be difficult for us to grasp now that bebop has come to represent high modernist intellectual rigor in contrast to the simplicity of the now-overexposed blues. But such are the ironies offered up by history.)

It now became fashionable for art students to denounce jazz; John Lennon said of jazz, for instance, "I think it is shit music, even more stupid than rock and roll. . . . Jazz never gets anywhere, never does anything, it's always the same and all they do is drink pints of beer."[39] In place of jazz, they began to exalt the new blues-based rock'n'roll of Chuck Berry, the first model for the Beatles, Rolling Stones, and Clapton. Then they began to look back to acquaint themselves with Berry's musical ancestors. Concerning this conversion, Clapton said:

> At first, I played exactly like Chuck Berry for six or seven months.
> You couldn't have told the difference when I was with the Yardbirds. Then I got into older bluesmen. Because he was so readily available, I dug Big Bill Broonzy; then I heard a lot of cats I had never heard before: Robert Johnson and Skip James and Blind Boy Fuller. I just finally got completely overwhelmed in this brand-new world. I studied it and listened to it and went right down in it and came back up in it.[40]

Although few of the British art-school students had previous experience with music, many of them acquired guitars and began learning to play—virtually in front of the indulgent coffee-house audiences who shared their enthusiasms and political associations.

In these various debates among English fans, neither side had a particularly clear sense of black culture in America; they used their musical allegiances to meet their own needs.[41] Yet it was significant that it was the music of black males they idolized, for African Americans were thought to have access to real (i.e., preindustrialized) feelings and community—qualities hard to find in a society that had so long stressed individuality and the mind/body split. Moreover, in contrast to what politicized art students regarded as the feminized sentimentality of pop music, blues seemed to offer an experience of sexuality that was unambiguously masculine. This was no mean consideration, for the English had regarded music-making as effeminizing for nearly 500 years.[42] Suddenly it was possible for British males to participate in music without the homophobic stigma of what Philip Brett has theorized as "musicality" attaching to them.[43] But the brand of masculinity that resulted from this identification with black music differed considerably from its model. As Ian Chambers has observed, the rebelliousness of the British bluesmen "tended to take the form of reducing the ironic cast of the blues to a blatant obsession with male sexuality."[44]

Meanwhile Mayall continued to mine the archives for earlier manifestations of blues and to recover obscure race records of the previous thirty years. Some of the old bluesmen were found to be still active as performers, mostly in urban clubs. Overnight Muddy Waters, Howling Wolf, B. B. King, Buddy Guy, and others became celebrities in England—an unanticipated turn of fate they were happy to exploit. For instance, Big Bill Broonzy, who had long played electric blues, converted back to acoustic and developed a "raw" style of delivery in order to satisfy this new audience's demand for ever-greater purity: "authenticity" became his ticket to commercial success.[45]

It was within this highly charged context that Keith Richards and Eric Clapton discovered the newly released Columbia LP of Robert

Johnson. As Richards said later, "To me Robert Johnson's influence—he was like a comet or a meteor that came along and, BOOM, suddenly he raised the ante, suddenly you just had to aim that much higher."[46] Clapton described his experience with Johnson's music this way: "It was as if I had been prepared to receive Robert Johnson, almost like a religious experience that started out with hearing Chuck Berry, then at each stage went further and deeper until I was ready for him."[47] To both, it was not only Johnson's extraordinary musicianship that drew them but also what they took to be his freedom from commercialism. As Clapton says,

> I played it, and it really shook me up because it didn't seem to me that he was particularly interested in being at all palatable, he didn't seem concerned with appeal at all. All the music I'd heard up till that time seemed to be structured in some way for recording. What struck me about the Robert Johnson album was that it seemed like he wasn't playing for an audience at all; it didn't obey the rules of time or harmony or anything—he was just playing for himself. It was almost as though he felt things so acutely he found it almost unbearable.[48]

What a place to encounter the "Who Cares If You Listen?" line![49]

Clapton passed through a number of British blues bands, working on his guitar skills and listening carefully to Johnson. Eventually he created the always already legendary band Cream with drummer Ginger Baker and bass player Jack Bruce. Cream was noted for its live performances, in which members of the band would improvise in response to audience feed-back—feed-back heightened for purposes of the Dionysian fervor cultivated in the late 1960s by hallucinogens. It was around this time that Clapton began to eclipse his idols, as the motto "Clapton is God" appeared scrawled on walls throughout Europe and North America. Although they created much of their own material, they also covered some traditional blues numbers, including Johnson's "Cross Road Blues."

Cream's version, titled "Crossroads," retains Johnson's lyrics, with a substitute verse (about taking his "rider" or lover to Rosedale) taken from another of Johnson's blues, "Traveling Riverside Blues":

I'm goin' down to Rosedale, take my rider by my side,
Goin' down to Rosedale, take my rider by my side,
We can still barrelhouse, baby, on the river side.[50]

And the model of Johnson's organizing riffs became indispensable to Cream's modus operandi. But the band replaces Johnson's eerie, strangulated riff in "Cross Road" with one that boasts a driving, propulsive beat and an insistent aeolian seventh-degree that announces their refusal of pop-oriented tonality. This riff returns throughout the song, pounding out the tonic whenever it appears.

Several aspects of Cream's performance depart more significantly from Johnson. First, their presentation of the blues pattern is absolutely regular, like the Chicago blues bands rather than Johnson. This is in part because of the presence of an ensemble and also because of the way blues practices had solidified by that time. One can't really imagine a rock band attempting to duplicate Johnson's erratic performance—at least not before the progressive rock bands of the 1970s and thrash metal groups of the 1980s.

Second, the structure of Cream's version articulates a brand of individuality in which self is pitted against society (even as it contributed to and drew from the sensibilities of the counterculture society of the 1960s). In Johnson's version, imagination is manifested in the particularities of his expression; he affirms the convention of proceeding through a series of identically shaped verses, but he signifies constantly throughout the entire number, forcing us to dwell on each moment, each detail as it comes. By contrast, the Cream recording minimizes expression within the verses in order to showcase the virtuosic solos for which Clapton became idolized, thereby reshaping the additive process of the blues to create an overarching formal trajectory. Clapton's solos operate like those in a concerto or bebop combo, as he strains forward in increasingly more extravagant figuration before yielding to the communal ritornello.[51]

. Two solo choruses occur after the verse about Rosedale; then after repeating that verse, Clapton pulls out the stops and plays three choruses that threaten to derail the song with his rebellious individualism. During the solos, Jack Bruce's walking bass contributes to the sense of instability and urgency. The return to the final verse about Willie Brown, which served as the chilling culmination in Johnson, here becomes an aftermath during which listeners can begin to wind down after the ferocious display of improvised pyrotechnics they have just witnessed. Cream pushes the envelope of Johnson's strophic organization, imposing on it the dynamic, climax-oriented shape typical of European-based narratives.[52]

Accordingly, the prominence of the vocal quality of Johnson's performance—even in his guitar playing—and his emphasis on the imagery of the lyrics have been inverted in Cream. Virtually everything in the Cream version revolves around the primacy of the instrumentals, especially in the riff and Clapton's individualistic solos. His singing is fairly perfunctory, even a shade self-conscious ("Crossroads" is the only song in which he contributed lead vocals on *Wheels of Fire*). And the staggering range of timbres employed throughout by Johnson—sonic evidence of his body's intimate engagement with the music—disappears except during the solos. Not too surprisingly, Cream has "hardened" the blues; those elements that signified the body in its vulnerability (whether in vocals, cross-rhythms, or timbral shadings) are exchanged for a driving beat, a narrative trajectory in the music, and the display of alienated Romantic virtuosity.[53]

Thus the priorities of the genre changed when it was adopted by British rockers—as they had, for that matter, when the blues passed from Bessie Smith to Robert Johnson. That the principal interests of the British differed from those of the African American musicians they initially idolized became clear when musicians and critics alike announced that they were ready to leave their black mentors behind and move forward into art rock. As Motown historian Dave Morse complained in 1971: "Black musicians are now implicitly regarded as precursors who, having taught the white men all they know, must gradually recede into the distance, as white progressive music, the simple lessons mastered, advances irresistibly into the future."[54] The mind/body split—temporarily suspended—returned, motivating the critical dismissal of black dance-oriented music: the British had received access to their bodies by means of their alignment with African American music; but after a point, they felt they had to rescue that music from the body.

When middle-class kids and British art students "universalized" blues by making it the vehicle for their own alienation, many black musicians chose to develop other modes of expression. For some of them, in any case, the blues had come to recall times of rural poverty and victimization—the genealogy sedimented into the blues had moved to the foreground for them, drowning out other registers of meaning. Thus it is no coincidence that rap musicians have worked to construct a different heritage, tracing their roots through sampling and quotation back not to the blues per se but to James Brown and soul—a genre of black music that emerged during the decade when white rockers arrogated the blues unto themselves. For African Americans the blues was always just one particular manifestation of a number of deeper elements that live on in other genres. It was never a fetish, but simply a vehicle for expression. When historical conditions changed, when it became reified, it could be left behind.

To be sure, the blues as a genre still exists intact. Many of the old bluesmen lionized in the 1960s—B. B. King, Buddy Guy—continue to play concerts.[55] Some of the 1920s blues queens, such as Alberta

Hunter, were rediscovered by feminist historians in the 1970s, and women's blues has enjoyed a rebirth with artists such as Etta James and Bonnie Raitt. Moreover, a neo-blues trend may have started with the emergence of younger musicians such as Robert Cray. Even those not identified with the blues continue to find it an invaluable point of reference, a repository from which they may draw gestures, moods, evocations of a variety of times past.

But the way we tell the history of the blues is often shaped by that period of British enthusiasm. Although the enterprise of British rock was certainly not untouched by the desire for commercial success, an ideology of noncommercial authenticity that first led Clapton and others to champion the blues permeated their self-images as rebels against capitalism. It continues to inform many of the rock critics who emerged at that same time as the historians, theorists, and arbiters of popular taste who justified this particular enterprise.

Yet whatever reservations one might harbor concerning that moment in blues history, it is now part of the permanent record. And some of its results were, in retrospect, quite startling. For instance, this fusion between African American models and British aesthetic priorities permitted the first truly international wave of English musical creativity since perhaps Elizabethan times. Moreover, it was in the wake of this fusion that the blues became inescapably a necessary chapter in the history of Western music: one could no longer even explain how white, European males came to compose the music they contributed without a detour through the Mississippi Delta.

This is not to suggest that black music deserves legitimacy only insofar it is found to be of use to Europeans or white Americans. Indeed, I would claim that the musical innovations that have most shaped people in the course of this century have principally come from African Americans, who have given the world a legacy that richly demands (and is finally receiving) attention in its own right. But it is hard to draw the line any longer between various strands of music in North

America and Europe, for they have shared the same geographical and temporal spaces, responded to the same historical conditions. And in the second half of the twentieth century, many prominent Western musicians—white as well as black—have come to identify themselves as descendants of African American traditions in addition to or rather than the classical canon. Thus the odd designation of black music as "non-Western," which might have seemed reasonable at one time, was no longer even remotely defensible after the 1960s.

There is no Hegelian reason why this should have happened. This merger occurred as a result of a number of unlikely circumstances— the technology of recording, which made possible (though not necessarily probable) the transmission of African American voices beyond their own times and places; the increasing obscurantism of the European tradition, which created a cultural vacuum; a political faction among British art school students who chose the blues as their symbol of defiance; the explosion of a global counterculture that depended on the demographics of the baby boom and the looming presence of an unpopular war. None of these or their impacts could have been predicted, nor was blues the necessary vehicle, even though the specific qualities of the blues drawn upon—its ability to galvanize community, engage emotions, and animate the body—indicate that the choice was not arbitrary either. Yet music history has always lurched along (I won't say advances) by just such circumstances: we impose the illusion of a smooth narrative unfolding only long after the fact.

In the next chapter, I want to examine one of those sequences in Western music history that seems to flow smoothest—the music of the Enlightenment—in terms that parallel those I have just brought to the blues. For it is not just the procedures of popular music that develop ad hoc according to unforeseen contingencies but also the most "purely musical" elements in the canon. Yet I hope to have established that this process of grabbing established conventions and arranging them according to the needs of the moment can be artistically powerful and culturally consequential—especially if we pay close attention to the signifying devices engaged in each tune as well as the historical contexts that make them meaningful. If we musicologists often have difficulty grasping how music and social conditions interact, if we still sometimes believe that adhering to conventions means the surrender of individuality and expression, we can learn a great deal by thinking blues.

CHAPTER 3

# What Was Tonality?

At first glance (and maybe second and third as well), eighteenth-century European art music would seem to have little in common with the blues. Not only do the musical practices themselves bear scant resemblance to one another, but the temporal, geographical, and social locations of the personnel involved—disenfranchised African Americans versus composers working under the patronage of Italian courts and German churches—demand radically different modes of historical analysis. Yet just as many artists during our own era have found the blues a compelling template for musical and cultural expression, so eighteenth-century musicians embraced with great enthusiasm the particular cluster of conventions we call tonality.

We know these conventions so well that we scarcely notice them except as technical devices, which is one reason I have chosen to put them up next to the blues. By juxtaposing these highly conventionalized discourses from two very distant cultural contexts, I propose to defamiliarize temporarily the musical premises we in musicology most often accept as "purely musical." As with the blues in the last chapter, I will ask how eighteenth-century procedures intersected with and helped to structure the social world in which they played active roles. My other reason is less arbitrary. Among the musical cultures to which we in

North America have access, none has influenced more profoundly our present day world than the blues and the European tonal repertory, and we need some idea of the social grounding of both in order to make sense of our own time.

Strange though it may seem, although musicology often assumes that tonality constitutes the foundation of Western music (we teach first-year students about music theory, *tout court*, by means of tonal principles), we also neglect many of the eighteenth-century repertories that most clearly enact its principles. Because our critical methods developed from philosophies of Romantic resistance, we prefer to focus our attention on pieces that rebel against tonal conventions: we whine over the vestiges of modality in the music of seventeenth-century composers and breathe a sigh of relief over the advent of composers such as Corelli, who figured out—*finally!*—how to be entirely tonal. But then we usually abandon them as soon as we have ascertained that they satisfy the minimal grammatical requirements, as though we were merely marking harmony exercises. Except for Bach and Mozart, who challenge us with the occasional enigmatic episode, it is primarily the convention-breakers of the nineteenth century who spark our analytical interest and goad us on toward further study.

Yet the deviations signify little if the norms they resist mean nothing. Whatever it was that got consolidated in the 1700s, its perceived power motivated the love/hate theatrics of Beethoven, Schubert, Wagner, and Mahler, as well as the strict prohibitions against its use by the twentieth century's avant-garde. In this chapter, I want to examine not the music of those who acted out against the hegemony of tonality but of those who inhabited it unapologetically, who first demonstrated what this new technology could accomplish.

The eighteenth century was a period of almost unparalleled confidence in the viability of a public sphere in which ideas could be successfully communicated, differences negotiated, consensus achieved: thus the concern with compiling encyclopedias and with codifying language, the arts, and even thought itself, as well as the widespread standardization and adoption of conventions. To be sure, some of the impulses to codify came from the top down, most obviously in the regulated cultural practices of absolutist courts. But people who identified with liberal causes also put a premium on intelligibility and the efficacy of shared discourses.

The question I want to pursue in the course of this chapter is why the particular musical conventions that crystallized during this period appealed so much to musicians and audiences of the Enlightenment. What needs did they satisfy, what functions did they serve, what kinds of cultural work did they perform? I will concentrate especially on tonality, the convention that undergirds and guarantees all the others, discussing how it constructed musical analogs to such emergent ideals as rationality, individualism, progress, and centered subjectivity. Far from merely reflecting their times, these musical procedures participated actively in shaping habits of thought on which the modern era depended. They resemble strongly many of the other modes of discourse and representation that stabilized during the eighteenth century and that continue to influence us, even today.

The fact that music theorists of the time did not by and large write about music in these terms should hardly surprise us: verbal accounts of "structures of feeling" often appear only long after the fact, if at all, even in the more explicitly representational arts.[1] To be sure, eighteenth-century theorists often addressed the rhetorical aspects of their music,[2] but their task was to offer guidelines for producing certain kinds of images and effects—not to explain what they meant. Further, Leonard Ratner and Wendy Allanbrook have demonstrated that eighteenth-century music relied heavily for intelligibility on "topics"—associations with dances, genres, and stylistic types.[3] Yet these *topoi*, though extremely important at the level of deliberate semiosis, rarely affect the dimensions of the music responsible for ensuring structural coherence, which is my concern here.

It might be objected that we should let these structures stand as exclusively formal arrangements. But to do so would be to continue to ignore the vast project of cultural formation they have enabled over the course of the last three hundred years. So long as we neglect to observe how this set of aesthetic practices encouraged our predecessors to understand the world and their very subjectivities in particular ways, we keep musical procedures detached from material history; if declaring music an autonomous realm was politically advantageous at one time, it has long since rendered music culturally trivial.[4] Moreover, so long as we refuse to understand the social premises of main stream European music, we will find it impossible to engage with other kinds of musics—even other kinds of European art music—except through radically different, incommensurate methods.

I want to address the question of metaphor here at the outset. Some scholars complain that metaphors interpose themselves between the listener and the pure experience of the music.[5] But I will claim (a claim familiar to other branches of cultural studies) that dominant cultural tropes influence the shaping of music itself.[6] They do not, in other words, qualify as "extramusical"; they are constitutive of the musical fabric at the most fundamental levels. The qualities I trace in this chapter preoccupied eighteenth-century cultural production and thought. They are precisely what was at stake during this period, no less in music than in political philosophy or literature.

As is the case with the blues, the general premises of eighteenth-century tonality are relatively easy to describe. The background of a tonal composition—itself the conventional linear descent of the sixteenth-century modal cadence—proceeds through a series of arrivals, beginning in the tonic key, moving through a few other keys, and returning finally home to the tonic. This background thereby traces a trajectory something like a quest narrative, with return to and affirmation of original identity guaranteed in advance. Whereas in the blues even narrative lyrics are rendered in strophes that minimize narrativity within the musical process, the linear unfolding of tonality almost always pursues a narrative-like series of dramatic events, regardless of the matter at hand. As anthropologists have pointed out, this kind of orientation with respect to time is so fundamental to those of us shaped by such forms that we tend to dismiss as primitive any cultural practices (whether blues or Philip Glass) based on other assumptions.[7]

In any given tonal composition, a succession of hierarchically related harmonies animates the moment-to-moment activity, producing both coherence and a sense of spontaneity. As we saw in chapter 1, these harmonies, based largely on the syntax associated with cadences, imply that closure is about to occur; they stimulate the expectation of or desire for that closure. Yet the composer need not—indeed, usually does not—deliver closure as soon as it is implied. Instead, various strategies (Schenker's middle-level operations)[8] serve to postpone that expected arrival; these strategies, although they initially withhold certainty, eventually confirm the belief that rational effort results in the attaining of goals. The self-motivated delay of gratification, which was necessary for the social world coming into being in the eighteenth century, worked on the basis of such habits of thought, and tonality teaches listeners how to live within such a world: how to project forward in time, how to wait patiently but confidently for the pay-off.

Within the relatively self-contained system of the tonal composition, events appear to generate themselves, to perform according to an abstract logic of cause and effect. Both surface and background are intensely goal oriented; they are, in other words, dynamic, progressive, rational, and driven by mechanisms that arouse and eventually satisfy desire. All moments of the composition participate in a hierarchy that guarantees the preeminence of the tonic. Even the most remote departure can be related logically back to the central core; indeed, the more remote the event, the more its eventual resolution confirms the power of the tonic's governing intelligence. As critics as different as Robert Morgan and Jean-François Lyotard have argued, the gap between the spontaneous-seeming events of the surface and the underlying structure produces the illusion of depth.[9] Thus the relationships between outward appearance and an unwavering core of subjective interiority—relationships that also preoccupied philosophers and literary figures at the time—find lucid articulation in tonal music.[10]

Again, I want to emphasize that this is not in some transhistorical sense "the way music is supposed to go," though it is often understood this way in metaphysical interpretations of Western culture. The historicity of tonality is clear not only to those who identify with (say) Indian ragas or free jazz, but also to anyone who relishes the music of the sixteenth or seventeenth centuries and who regrets the discontinuation of a whole range of formal options in favor of this one package of conventions, which were designed to deliver a particular set of effects; those other options worked perfectly well as means of structuring time and subjectivity.[11] But as cultural priorities came to focus almost obsessively on progress, rationality, intelligibility, quests after goals, and the illusion of self-contained autonomy, eighteenth-century musicians came to concentrate on this single basic procedure.

Once the listener has accepted the premises of tonality, any specific manifestation of it seems virtually natural—as though it operates without cultural intervention: tonality erases its ideology as it unfolds. A more perfect analog to emerging Enlightenment ideals—reason, purposeful advancement, the compatibility of social order and inner feelings, the possibility of self-generation—would be difficult to imagine. To the extent that we still embrace these ideals, the music of the eighteenth century can still appear to speak to us directly. We experience that world as unmediated reality when we listen; we forget that these patterns were historically produced.

The fact that eighteenth-century tonal compositions follow a more or less standard set of procedures does not suggest that they are all alike—or even that the tonal dimension of each piece always means or accomplishes the same thing. As was the case with the blues, many other musical elements enter the mix as well, and these particularize, inflect, and sometimes even destabilize what the tonal aspects of the piece would appear to suggest. Indeed, tonality always serves as part of the expressive apparatus, as well as provides the formal framework. Although its conventional aspects help it to communicate intelligibly without apparent intervention from outside the music itself, they are still living parts of the complex, always subject to negotiation.

In the remainder of this chapter, I will visit four moments in eighteenth-century music—not with the goal of creating a comprehensive history but in order to examine several ways in which tonality can be seen to operate as both form *and* content. My selection of examples—drawn from works by Alessandro Scarlatti, Vivaldi, J. S. Bach, and Mozart—deliberately goes against the accepted periodization in musicology, which labels the first half of the century as Baroque, the last couple of decades as Classic. Of course, all such groupings (including mine) heighten or suppress similarities and differences in order to justify artificial boundaries between styles. But I have always found the tradition of identifying the highly ordered music of the eighteenth century with the Baroque especially problematic: recall, for instance, that Handel composed for the same people who read the journalistic criticism of Addison and Steele. When I teach survey courses, I prefer to deal with the whole of the eighteenth century as the era of tonality— tonality understood as the enactment of the Enlightenment priorities already enumerated above. This mode of periodization suggests an alternative historical treatment from the ones we usually follow, as it presents a set of overriding cultural beliefs fleshed out to very different ends by its various eighteenth-century practitioners.

Just as the women who introduced the blues got marginalized by a mythology that wanted to locate the origins of the genre in the rural Delta, so musicological accounts of the Italians who standardized tonal processes have tended to get undervalued for the sake of a German-oriented historiography. If my previous chapter insisted on featuring Bessie Smith, this one will highlight (to an inordinate extent, some might claim) Antonio Vivaldi. And while I would not want to exalt either Smith or Vivaldi as an "author" operating outside the constraints of cultural practice, I do believe that both altered permanently the course of musical style by virtue of the imaginative changes they rang on basic conventions. For conventions do not take hold and get perpetuated simply because they are somehow meant to be; someone has to demonstrate their efficacy, their exceptional potential as cultural resources. If neither Smith nor Vivaldi invented their respective genres, they inhabited them so compellingly as to spawn many generations of followers.

I want to begin with an example that illustrates how early eighteenth-century tonality works to produce a particular construction of the self. It comes from that most convention-bound of genres, *opera seria*, which organized everything from aria-format to dramaturgy according to established regulations. Although this ritualized set of procedures has provoked the scorn of contemporaneous and present-day critics alike,[12] its prestige and dominance throughout the eighteenth century prove that it engaged successfully with crucial issues of the time. Some of the cultural work it performed was, to be sure, legislated by authorities: opera seria was in part a response by literati in Italianate courts to the neo-platonic discipline of the arts at Versailles; it was an attempt at cleaning up the flamboyance of the plots and musical procedures characteristic of Venetian public opera. Nevertheless, audiences clearly derived pleasure from these rigid spectacles, even as they lurched from formal aria to formal aria.

Among its other functions, the genre operated as a showcase for displaying the power of the new music to represent within rational form the whole spectrum of human affections. Its featured arias purported to make audible the internal workings of the soul, codified in the manner of Charles LeBrun's somewhat earlier systematized charts of faces depicting the passions.[13] Such artifacts celebrated the triumph of reason by demonstrating that even the most extreme of emotions could be captured and reproduced through modern discourses: the inner self no longer withheld secrets from cognition. Confidence in mimesis for mu-

sicians reached its peak in opera seria's succession of arias—all following the same format, yet each offering a strikingly different image of
interiority. The uniform packaging both attested to rational control
and reined in the erratic aspects of earlier practices.

As was the case with French art forms, opera seria had a didactic dimension: it held up as ideals characters who succeeded in imposing
control over their behaviors, expressions, and feelings.[14] For along with
the ability to represent unruly emotions through civilized forms came
the possibility of new, carefully regulated social relations and even rationally constituted subjectivities. Reason thereby promised to extend
its domain down into the innermost recesses of the self.[15]

Of course, the composers of opera seria did not invent an expressive
language out of nothing; they drew on a 200-year tradition that
stretched from Josquin and the sixteenth-century madrigalists to the
composers of earlier opera for their affective codes. Yet it would be a
mistake to assume the smooth linear development of expressive devices
and their premises. As soon as the potential for representing interiority
appeared in the sixteenth century, the possibility of inhabiting a space
not yet colonized by codes became a prevalent obsession. By the end of
that century, the consensus that had marked the musical practices of
the High Renaissance had been profoundly eroded by deliberately deviant strategies—especially in the works of extreme mannerists such as
Gesualdo. But early opera picked up the shards of the vocabulary developed within the context of the madrigal and fashioned the semblance of rhetorically inflected, impassioned speech from it. With the
advent of opera seria in the late seventeenth century, social encoding
had become once again not only acceptable but even cause for cultural
celebration, for its affirmative practices demonstrated society's triumph
over those pockets of resistant feeling that had apparently overwhelmed structures of communal reason (albeit quite different structures) a century earlier.

The Italians who composed, performed, and attended opera seria
contributed little to the explicit theorizing of their musical practices

during this time. They left that task to German intellectuals of the *Aufklärung* (Johann Mattheson, for instance), who recognized in opera seria the successful rationalization of the passions, and they produced elaborate lexicons detailing the construction in music of affective types.[16] We may, of course, contest what these writers regarded as the transparency of the musical discourse they studied, as we can also question Enlightenment confidence in language itself as an unproblematic mode of public exchange. What seems undeniable, however, is the sense of cultural exaltation revealed both in opera seria's musical demonstrations and in documents of the *Affektenlehre*. Musicians believed that they had finally perfected a vocabulary for representing the universals of subjective feelings within a universally accessible system of social encoding, and they could thus provide its audiences with laudable models not only of external behavior but of rationally construed interiority. At a single triumphant moment, they brought both musical process and feelings under the umbrella of social reason and consensus.

But it is not only the manifest content of these arias that bears witness to the glorification of reason in opera seria but also their formal logic. Italian composers in the generation just before the advent of opera seria often delighted in defying closure. In arias that unfolded in an asymmetrical ABB′ format, composers such as Alessandro Stradella frequently infused the second presentation of B materials with unexpected energies, flirting with the possibility that excess feeling might overwhelm anticipated structural bounds—the guarantee of musical reason.[17] By contrast, the A section of a da capo aria returns exactly as the last section of the ABA form: any disruption is multiply resolved—the tonally contrasting B section is buttressed on either side by statements of A, and dissonances within the A section are laid to rest both by the definitive conclusion of its first presentation and then by its literal reiteration after the B section (the second A section is not even notated but is merely signaled by the words "da capo," or "from the top").

Recall, however, that singers typically tempered this formal rigidity by adding effusive ornamentation during the repeated presentation of

A—a practice that relocated manifestations of excess to a different musical register. In effect, the syntactical level remained securely rational, allowing the virtuoso singer to challenge (in ways that appalled devotees of French classicist decorum) but eventually to embrace underlying reason. Thus despite the importation by literary reformers of certain aspects of neo-platonism, opera seria operated as a fusion, an ongoing negotiation between formal propriety and Italianate exuberance, with the most dramatic confrontations occurring at the site of the *performed* aria.

One of the principal musical technologies for performing this rational order was the newly consolidated version of tonality, which possessed both the flexibility necessary to produce viable depictions of the various passions and also a hierarchy of relationships that drew all moments of the composition together into a single goal-oriented network. Far from "universal," this device for prolonging a unified trajectory through a standardized set of modulations appeared only late in the seventeenth century, along with other genres (e.g., the novel) that began to trace narratives of centered subjectivity. For the duration of an aria (or a contemporary sonata movement by, say, Corelli), all activity seems to operate under the control of a single governing impulse. But because this process tends to remain unnoticed (it mobilizes the more evident dimensions of content while deflecting attention away from itself), it impresses itself all the more powerfully on the ways listeners structure their worlds. Both the affective codes of the *Affektenlehre* and the "purely musical" order of tonality count as conventions of eighteenth-century representation; both operate to affirm the ascent of reason in its ability finally to contain (but also to construct) human emotions; both worked to inscribe admiring listeners into specifically eighteenth-century habits of rationality.

The dramatic turning point in Alessandro Scarlatti's opera *Griselda* (1721) is a da capo aria sung by the title character. As Apostolo Zeno's libretto presents the story, Griselda—the shepherdess who became queen—has been exiled from the palace by her husband, the king, in response to complaints from the populace. The king, who trusts in Griselda's essential nobility and constancy, devises a series of tests for her without letting her know why he is subjecting her to such unrelenting abuse. She protests none of them, except for one final humiliation: he demands that she submit to the desires of the opera's villain, Ottone. When her marital fidelity to her husband runs into conflict with his explicit command, she disobeys his decree—even under the threat of death to herself and her son. Only at this point does the king call a halt to his charade; he restores her beneficently to the throne, this time with the blessing of the people.

The aria in question occurs at the moment of greatest duress for Griselda. The malignant Ottone has seized Griselda's son and has just delivered an ultimatum: either she gives herself to him or he will murder the child—by order, he claims, of the king. Faced with this impossible choice, she almost loses her powers of articulate speech as she exclaims, "Figlio! Tiranno! O Dio! Dite che far poss'io?" (Son! Tyrant! O God! Tell me, what can I do?). The broken quality of this fragmentary utterance, which sometimes more closely resembles recitative than formal aria, attests to her horror. Yet if the surface of the aria gives us an image of her distraught state, its formal unfolding reveals that she gradually overcomes her ordeal by means of her inner integrity. Where speech falters, tonality comes to the rescue, proving that even in a situation this extreme, Griselda's reason still maintains its sovereignty and control. Far from having shattered her sense of herself as centered and self-reliant, Ottone's persecution only reinforces her resolve. As she calls his bluff, defying him to carry out the execution, she wins this round in their ongoing struggle.

To render this text, Scarlatti must manage two dimensions of representation: the specific affect appropriate to the moment and the rational circumscription of that affect. Before the voice enters, we hear the instrumental accompaniment, which forgoes a formal ritornello in keeping with the urgency of the situation. It does, however, set forth the principal key—E♭ major—and the general affective realm of the aria. The violin lines present an image of agitation, punctuated with the swirling *passaggi* sometimes associated in music of this time with vengeful lightning bolts, and most of the pitches are repeated, contributing a degree of tenacity as well as the driving rhythms of rage. Presumably we are to hear in this accompaniment Griselda's inner condition, especially in the bass, which advances steadily underneath her frenetic utterances and guides her securely toward her (tonal and dramatic) goal.

Up against the backdrop of the accompaniment, Griselda's melody stammers: her first word, "figlio," appears on the weak part of the measure, as though she blurts it out involuntarily; and while "tiranno" occupies a strong metric position and begins to trace an ascending line to the mediant, G , "O Dio" falls dejectedly to the G an octave lower. A sequence follows that once again leads up from tonic to second degree before sticking. At this point, she tries to decide on a course of action: she moves tentatively toward the dominant in measure 6, the subdominant in measure 8, only to hover indecisively in measure 10 on "Che far poss'io?" But suddenly after all that hesitation, she gathers her faculties, nails the high G that had seemed beyond her grasp, mounts resolutely onward to B♭, and delivers a virtual slam-dunk into the tonic cadence. Note that the lyrics do not register any kind of resolution here—Griselda merely sings the word "tiranno" again twice. Yet Scarlatti's music has her rising defiantly above her quandary; she overcomes all obstacles while maintaining her integrity (Ex. 3.1).

The middle section of the aria, which serves to give us greater insight into Griselda's interiority, pursues a similar course. While contemplating her maternal love, she vacillates again among possible keys, repeatedly almost succumbing to the melancholy of C minor or opting for the temporary yet illusory comfort of A♭ major (m. 17). But at the last moment, she summons her strength of purpose. She converts the melodic D in measure 20, which is poised to resolve to C minor, to an unyielding fifth degree and forces an unexpected cadence in G minor, which pivots back immediately to her outraged opening section.[18]

Example 3.1: Scarlatti, *La Griselda,* "Figlio! Tiranno!"

Example 3.1 (*continued*)

mor di _ ma-dre a-man-te    mi squar-cia,    me squar-cia in pet-to,    mi squar-cia in pet-to il cor, _    il

solo

cor, ___    ma il    cor trop-po co - stan - te    co - si squar-cia - to an-cor, co - si squar-cia - to an-

cor vin - ce, vin - ce, via - ce il suo af-fan - - - no,    vin-ce il suo af-fan - no.

Da capo

After concluding her reiteratation of the opening section, she triumphantly exits the stage—in keeping with one of the most gratifying of opera seria conventions. In conquering her own doubts and finding the confidence to pursue tonal continuity, she also somehow satisfies the dramatic situation: Ottone puts away his sword.

Modern listeners often complain that opera seria lacks both dynamic change and any sense of long-term identity in its characterizations. For although Griselda proceeds through many crises over the course of the opera, she remains constant—fundamentally unchangeable, yet also *interchangeable* with other such characters who similarly exhibit a wide range of recognizable attitudes. Depending on the situation, she takes on and sheds affects as though they were costumes, in keeping with the static, hierarchical conception of identity within the court circles for which opera seria was composed. Yet without this technology for creating analogs of inner feelings, the dynamic model of the subject that emerges later in the century—a subject that maintains some modicum of identity while continually developing—could not have occurred.

The advantages of tonal conventions are quite apparent in this brief aria. Tonality gives Scarlatti's character the flexibility to express a series of passions (outrage, doubt, hesitation, sorrow, illusion, decisiveness) and also an all-embracing, rational sense of purpose. It is difficult not to celebrate Griselda's ability to pull her conflicting emotions under one tonal trajectory, thus displaying the centered subjectivity—the belief in the unshakability of that inner core—which is still one of our favorite myths, poststructuralism notwithstanding.

Although tonality developed first largely as a mode of representation within opera, its ability to project a compelling sense of coherence throughout an entire composition also attracted composers of instrumental music. Corelli's sonata movements, for instance, make use of the same devices as those in the example by Scarlatti to present affective nuances on the one hand and rational order on the other. When Corelli began amplifying and punctuating crucial dramatic moments in his sonatas with a larger ensemble to create the concerto grosso (a technique he may have learned, incidentally, by playing violin in Stradella's 1675 oratorio *San Giovanni Battista*), he continued to draw on the model of the opera aria.

Although Corelli, Torelli, and others explored the potentialities of concerto terracing, it was Vivaldi who standardized the Baroque concerto into the format that set the terms of composition for years to come. Vivaldi's contribution involves his having taken the tonal procedure developed as a vehicle for representing subjectivity and altering it so that it enacts a dramatically compelling model of self/group interactions. That is, the logic designed to regulate the centered self comes to preside over a particular vision of a social world that negotiates between individual virtuosity and consensus.

Vivaldi's concerto format follows a linear trajectory—a quasi-narrative procedure that alternates passages of dynamic striving toward the next key with moments of consolidation. According to the premises of the genre, both dynamic and consolidating functions prove indispensable, and both are already implied within the ritornello: a microcosm of the movement that establishes key, motives, affective terrain, and even the fundamental tension between the desiring and stabilizing aspects of tonality that will seem to generate the piece. As the concerto unfolds, a division of labor emerges: the soloists take most of the responsibility for motion and progress—they effect modulations and display idiosyncratic brilliance—while the group enters to acknowledge and celebrate the successive arrivals achieved by the soloists.

Because of the absence of verbal text, the concerto appears to make itself up out of its own materials. Vivaldi accomplishes this relatively easily through devices inherited from opera: a dependable vocabulary for representing affect and the powerful set of expectations provided by tonality, which connect surface, middle, and background levels in ways that resemble necessity. The rationality that governs the aria through its tonal trajectory embraces the series of exchanges between the large group and the showcased soloists. Throughout any given movement, the demands for progressive motion and collective stabilization remain in balance. If the eccentricities of the soloists require the safety net of the group for coherence, the group relies on the soloists' dynamism to avoid stagnation. On occasion the group enacts dramatic shifts, independent of the soloists, and the soloists sometimes prove stable: the actual playing out of the process—while easy to follow—remains pliable, subject to the imaginative whim of the composer.

Tonality underwrites several dimensions of the concerto: the stability of the tutti, the plotted trajectory of the structure, and the various means of simulating dramatic suspense, dynamic action, and closure. Within that framework is enacted a specific kind of social world that allows equally for collaboration and individuality—an arrangement that permits both to exist, to work together toward progress, reason, consensus, freedom of expression, and long-range goals. And although the modulatory succession follows a newly conventionalized schema, the flexibility of the movement's unfolding (how long it stays in each place, how it makes each seem a product of will, reason, effort) invites us to perceive each moment as sui generis. That this model arose in Venice rather than in a French-influenced absolutist court is probably not coincidental. And once forged, the concerto could circulate, spreading its influence—musical and ideological—wherever it went, even into the heavy metal of the 1980s.[19]

The wordlessness of the procedure permits it to seem as though it operates independently of any cultural agenda, and this becomes a fiercely held premise of later instrumental genres. Yet far from escaping the ideological, Vivaldi's concertos make palpable one of the most cherished tenets of eighteenth-century thought: that individual will and social consensus are compatible—indeed, that the new progressive society requires the actions of imaginative, risk-taking agents, while those agents in turn rely on the approval of a supportive environment. It is largely tonality's cause-and-effect qualities that weave these potentially antagonistic forces together into a single coherent trajectory, so that we experience as virtually inevitable both the exuberance of the solos and the periodic arrivals at consensus. Even if it proves difficult (if not impossible) to implement in the real world, this is still one of our most cherished models of social interaction.

In his concertos, Vivaldi works extensively with tensions between the collective and individuals, with the ritornello usually aligned with stability, the soloists with virtuosity and the kind of progressive desire characteristic of seventeenth-century tonality. This duality serves several functions simultaneously. Formally, it lays the groundwork for extraordinary expansion: if seventeenth-century musical procedures had to move on toward the next key area immediately after a cadence, the ritornello permits the piece to prolong a moment of repose within a single key before it has to start modulating onward. If the soloists continue to behave very much in the style of, say, Stradella's Susanna in their striving, the tutti insert islands of relative stability—indeed, stability of the sort we now identify more as the essence of tonality than the images of restless desire that precede it historically. And motivic identity becomes an increasingly important device, in part as a way of holding these longer and longer pieces together as units.

But all these formal innovations also bring into play—and are brought into play by—the emerging cluster of classic eighteenth-century binary oppositions between, for instance, collective and individual or stability and progress. If seventeenth-century procedures seemed to trace the trajectory of desire itself, the interest in motivic play in the eighteenth century attaches the action to ersatz personae. In a certain sense, we exchange the explorations of apparently unmediated Mannerist interiority offered by the seicento for the dramatic representations of selves engaged in fundamental social tensions typical of the Enlightenment. This restructuring of what had been the continuous unfolding of the tonal process by means of culturally loaded binary oppositions greatly raises the stakes in the outcome of pieces, and the kind of emplotment Paul Ricoeur associates with narrative forms becomes an important dimension of both composition and hearing.[20]

My example is Op. 3, no. 8 in A minor, from the collection *l'Estro armonico* (1715). To the jaded ears of those of us who have been subjected to too many of these apparently interchangeable pieces on public radio (especially through the sewing-machine renditions that flooded the airwaves during the 1970s), this collection offers nothing *but* convention. Yet the modus operandi crystallized by Vivaldi in *l'Estro armonico* accomplished a great deal, and it richly deserved the cultural clout it acquired. Vivaldi was not the only composer to revel in the iterability of his convention: this is, after all, the collection that so influenced Bach that he transcribed several of its pieces (including this one) for his own purposes. Indeed, as we will see in the next section, Bach self-consciously internalized Vivaldi's procedures and deployed them, in fusion with many other influences, for the rest of his career. Yet from the point of view of the late seventeenth century, there was nothing obvious or natural about Vivaldi's model. What cultural work did it enable that it should have dominated culture in the first half of the eighteenth century and beyond?

First, Vivaldi sets out with remarkable clarity the background tonal progression that had started life as a linear cadence pattern but that now stretches out to grant coherence to a full ninety-three measures. He marks each step along the way with a dramatic event that grabs our attention. As in many modal compositions and earlier moments of expansion in the seventeenth century, the fifth degree extends over the half of the movement, sustained variously by the tonic (A minor), the relative major (C major, mm. 32–43), and a brief nod to the minor dominant (E minor, mm. 44–47). The linear descent to the fourth degree occurs in measure 48, and the return to tonic, which initiates the completion of the progression, begins in measure 62.

| $\hat{5}$— | $\hat{5}$— | $\hat{5}$ | $\hat{4}$ | $\hat{3}\to\to\to\hat{1}$ |
|---|---|---|---|---|
| A minor→ | C major→ | E minor→ | D minor→ | A minor |
| 1–32 | 32–43 | 44–47 | 48–62 | 62–93 |

My schematic chart indicates that Vivaldi's movement satisfies the basic requirements for coherent tonal backgrounds—a background that guarantees the rationality of whatever happens within its scope. But the chart scarcely explains why anyone should care. Moreover, those of us accustomed to far longer degrees of expansion—movements by Beethoven, for instance, that sustain their logic over the course of twenty-minute spans—may hear Vivaldi's efforts as primitive. A seventeenth-century musician, however, would no doubt be stunned by how Vivaldi manages to stay in a single key for thirty-two measures: how he keeps interest from flagging and how he enacts the rhetoric of the background descent over the course of so long a piece. And this seems a more productive perspective from which to examine Vivaldi than one that takes tonal expansion and its attendant forms for granted.

The ritornello contains within itself a wealth of materials, each with a distinct rhetorical purpose closely tied to its grammatical function (Ex. 3.2). It begins with a forceful gesture that establishes the key through a forthright cadential alternation, followed by sweeping scales and galloping rhythms that spell, in the lexicons of the time, passionate (if rationally controlled) rage.[21] Although the chords alternate securely between tonic and dominant, the melody and harmony interact in such a way as to tilt the energy forward, as if in search of a place where arrivals in the tune will meet strong, root-position functions in the bass. Segment B (mm. 4–5) pauses for a breather; it hovers between dominant and tonic as the upper strings toss back and forth an auxiliary motive—a motive that makes no harmonic commitments (which contributes to its versatility) but that maintains a sense of restlessness as it holds in place like a race horse before the starting gun.

The music breaks out of this impasse as the upper strings seize the auxiliary and twist it into a motive that achieves harmonic motion, through the circle of fifths. The pent-up frustration generated in the first segments finds release through this most rational and predictable of progressions: a progression that suggests productive activity but that frequently (as in this case) spirals through a number of possible areas before looping back to where it began—to the tonic. This illusion of motion satisfies a desire to press forward, a desire generated by the ritornello's earlier configurations; yet its apparent motion returns immediately to reinforce tonal order. A dominant pedal in measure 9 announces impending cadence, though closure is no sooner implied than it too is deferred through melodic arpeggios that refuse to conform—even to the point of straining erratically against the meter. When it occurs in measure 13, the cadence is too sudden and another approach to closure appears, this one marked by Neapolitan inflections (i.e., a flatted second degree in the violin sighs) and a chromatic bass—the kinds of unconventional harmonies that conventionally bespeak pathos—before both melody and harmony join to produce a strong, unequivocal arrival on A.

What Vivaldi does supremely well in his ritornello is to harness the urgency of "mere" dominant/tonic cadential patterns, endow them with striking motivic profiles so they project independent identities despite their simple cadential basis, then elide the anticipated ending of one with the novelty of the next. To distract the listener from potential tedium (the music stays in a single key for the length of the ritornello), he offers the impression of rapidly shifting variety; yet this variety achieves coherence by virtue of the tonality that underwrites it. Listeners can surrender themselves to the dazzling sequence of surface events without ever having to worry about direction or location.

As a matter of strategy, Vivaldi saves his ritornello's most affectively charged segments for last (mm. 9–16). After having smacked into the dominant preparation, he distends it far past its functional duration while the violins writhe with asymmetrical rhythmic groupings, as though seeking escape from bonds. Then, in measure 14, just after what could serve as a final cadence and when syntactical certainty is at its highest, he splices in that moment of Neapolitan disquiet. Only after this unexpected insertion does he reaffirm his original destination with a conclusive cadence. If we now tend to hear the sequence of events as

Example 3.2: Vivaldi, Concerto Op. 3, No. 8: opening ritornello

natural, it is because of the harmonic security that anchors it—and also because Vivaldi's methods became such standard practice that we don't hear them anymore.

Yet Vivaldi's success owes less to his harmonic than to his rhythmic skills. I am not referring here to the constant sixteenth notes that inspired the clockwork performances of the 1970s (to which some listeners cling as an aural security blanket) but to his judicious alternation of moments of tension and release, his uncanny sense of weights and balances. If the cadence in measure 13 had been commensurate with the pent-up energy accumulated over the dominant pedal in measures 9–12, the final segment of the ritornello would have sounded tacked on. As it stands, however, the ear demands something more after the perfunctory cadence in measure 13—even if what it gets is the Neapolitan moan that stands between it and a cadence extensive enough to absorb the momentum of the previous sixteen measures. The impression that this additional segment is not only tolerable but *necessary* results from Vivaldi's deft manipulation of phenomenological time. Such rhythmic strategies convince listeners of inevitability without actual predictability; coupled with the cause/effect illusion of cadential harmonies, they account for the dominance of tonal procedures during the Age of Reason.

Throughout the movement, Vivaldi stresses motivic identity. His motivic redundancy allows him to use any one of the ritornello segments at different moments throughout the movement and yet maintain a strong sense of formal connectedness among his tutti. From Vivaldi's works onward, reiterated motives will seem to guarantee the autonomy of a movement—both its difference from surrounding movements and its internal integrity—far more than the background syntax that sufficed for the shorter pieces of the seventeenth century. Put differently, as the linear progression retreats further and further away from the surface with expansion, motivic links assume the task of marking a piece's identity over the course of its duration; the motivicism often associated with Beethoven already comes into play at this

much earlier stage. Yet because the ritornello already contains segments that serve very different functions (qualities variously of opening, hovering, traveling, and closing), it can accommodate itself to any
musical or dramatic situation.

Although the ritornello includes both stable and dynamic elements,
it does not achieve any modulations: its circle of fifths only suggests the
potential for motion and whets the listener's appetite for action. But Vivaldi defers movement beyond the tonic to the efforts of the soloists.
When they enter, however, they start tentatively—first teetering between tonic and subdominant, then creeping downward by step in the
bass to a by-now redundant confirmation of tonic. Nothing ventured,
nothing gained, and the tutti breaks in with its Neapolitan segment,
announcing final closure before the soloists have even begun. Yet the
very fact of the tutti's difference in sonority prevents that premature
announcement of conclusion from sticking. When the soloists return in
measure 25, they grope as before until the first violin takes charge in
measure 30, its higher-energy virtuosity apparently pulling out of the
stagnation that had prevailed. In measure 32 (the moment when all
previous patterns had fallen passively to E in the bass), the smaller
group enacts a move to the G, the dominant of C major. Without the
G♯, the piece ceases to gravitate back to A minor.

Once in the domain of C major, a series of affirmations occurs, each
lending greater solidity to this new key. The solo violin enacts several
rather teasing approaches to cadence, establishing the listener's expectation of C while postponing its actual arrival until measure 37. The
entire ensemble enters on that cadence, reinforces the soloists in sustaining C, then moves into the circle-of-fifths segment of the ritornello,
sharing the action with the soloists who made it possible.

As before, the circle of fifths loops around to its point of origin in
measure 42. But we no sooner arrive back on C than the music gets
stuck. All instruments reiterate the thunderbolt scales from the ritornello's first measure, which churn up the energy level toward no obvious end. Suddenly, with no more warning than that simultaneous

paralysis and ominous rise in rhythmic tension, the context veers onto a preparation for E minor—the third of the three keys available for sustaining the fifth degree. It would be easy enough to usher in that move from C major to E minor as a gentle, melancholy shading, but Vivaldi treats it here as a catastrophe—rather as though that cascade of C-major scales had put too much pressure on the San Andreas Fault and precipitated a disaster. The large ensemble and the soloists together accomplish this calamity and its rueful arrival on E minor in measure 47.

But the arrival on E cannot compete dramatically with what follows immediately in its wake. In modal music, the descent from the fifth degree to the fourth often sounds abrupt and even traumatic, and Vivaldi produces this effect particularly well in his breathtaking turn-around from the cruel cadence on E minor to a parallel one on D minor in the very next measure (Ex. 3.3). In essence, he simply yanks the entire structure down a peg with only the slightest of contrapuntal niceties (a $V^{6/5}$ of D minor a mere eighth note in duration) to cushion the drop. Just as the ear begins to accommodate itself to the reality of E, Vivaldi demands that it adjust to D. On one level, this move seems extraordinarily arbitrary—absent are the familiar gradual shifts in surface harmonies that lead as though by natural logic from one key center to another. Indeed, it sounds like a violation of the tonal contract: if Vivaldi can hurl us from E to D in a single measure, why not anything at any time? Yet what he has done is to thrust the background progression suddenly to the foreground without the expansion to which we have become accustomed. We may have forgotten the exigencies of the modal descent; but here it is, fully exposed as a structural node as it might have been a century earlier in a *Passamezzo Antico*—an improvisatory pattern that shares this moment's effect of a willful, unadorned descent from $\hat{5}$ to $\hat{4}$.[22]

The key of D minor lasts for quite a long time, given the unceremonious coup with which it took over the piece. Vivaldi greets the arrival on D with a sudden hush, as unsupported violins move hesitantly to inhabit the new key. Upon their cadence in measure 51, the tutti enters,

Example 3.3: Vivaldi, Concerto Op. 3, No. 8: mm. 44–48

crowning this moment with the ritornello's most powerful gesture and implying the possibility of raising D minor to a formal status rivaling the opening key. This elevation of D minor continues as the soloists explore the new key through the figuration, auxiliary pattern, and slow harmonic rhythm that characterized the moments of tense apprehension in the ritornello. But in measure 62—just when D minor seems about to consolidate its reign with a cadence—Vivaldi pounces instead on a dominant preparation to A minor, where he stays for the remainder of the movement. For this cadence, he gives us, as we might have expected, the closing material from the ritornello—only it sounds like the wrong key, like another imposition of sheer will.

But, of course, it's actually the *right* key: the return to the tonic that spells the goal for tonal compositions. Vivaldi has worked hard to position this most predictable of arrivals in such a way as to make it sound alien. A series of events acclimatizes us gradually to the fact that we are, in fact, back in the tonic: that slow, groping entrance of the soloists as before, then the opening segment of the ritornello, expanded by another appearance of the soloists, the heightened energy of which always threatens further modulations. Yet the circle of fifths leads back to its point of departure and proceeds to the Neapolitan closing materials. Just when we ought to quit, however, the solo violins break in one last time with the slow-motion figuration with which they elaborated D minor. Only at their cadence in measure 90 does the ritornello answer and conclude the movement once and for all.

Vivaldi's contemporaries often regarded his music with distaste (even as they shamelessly pilfered from it the elements they found palatable), because his personal eccentricity and his virtuosity bled over into his compositions: the dynamic impulse of his procedures often strain against the formal plan designed to contain them. Not surprisingly, others preferred to balance ritornello and soloist with greater symmetry, thus reining in the exuberance of seventeenth-century striving with the architectural proclivities of court culture.

But Vivaldi did not operate within the administered *bon goût* of the court: often at odds with his employers, who found him difficult to control, he owed his fame to the tourist trade that brought audiences to Venice to hear dazzling performers and to the commercial print industry that circulated *l'Estro armonico* far beyond his own bailiwick. Alas, latter-day formal descriptions of Vivaldi often sound more like the trickle-down versions by his envious contemporaries than his own idiosyncratic compositions, which offended sensibilities even as their international success challenged his rivals to appropriate at least the semblance of his models.[23]

I have discussed Vivaldi's strategies with vocabulary borrowed from treatments of narrative, because his music constantly dramatizes alternatives, obstacles, achievements, surprises, and reversals as he moves through his modulatory background. If these moments are performed dramatically, listeners will wonder "what next?!" throughout the duration of the movement: his strategies took the standard operating procedure of the time and sutured in listeners through strategies that gave it the roller-coaster contour of action movies. Moreover, seemingly innocuous details (for instance, the Neapolitans) turn out to operate as plot markers; Vivaldi rewards our attentiveness by making these details appear crucial to the narrative unfolding of the movement. Finally, if at first the tutti and adventure-seeking soloists seem quite alien from one another, Vivaldi has them perform a reconciliation: not only do they prove compatible, but the two forces actually appear to work together in their achievement of the tonal trajectory.

Within this tonal process, Vivaldi performs the emplotted interaction between two forces initially quite dissimilar, puts them through a series of crises, and brings them eventually to a kind of détente. And this is what Ricoeur suggests is the cultural purpose of narrative. Despite all the apparent upheavals of fortune and affect, the standard tonal schema holds everything together as though causally. And conversely, despite the standard tonal schema that underwrites the piece,

Vivaldi makes all his moves appear both fresh and meaningful; his arrangement situates all these conventional moments in ways that allow them to accrue significance.

It is not too surprising that Vivaldi's formulation should have made converts of so many other composers, including J. S. Bach. Soon after transcribing this and others of Vivaldi's concertos, Bach adopted this model as his standard universe, revising everything he knew—even the Lutheran chorale and the fugue—in accordance with its logic. Yet tonality had no metaphysical status within Bach's symbolic economy. He recognized very well its secular origins and its constructedness: he had to work too hard to convert his practice over for it to have appeared natural.[24] And his awareness of its means of construction permitted him to play with contradictions, to exaggerate some components separate from others, to call it into question even as he bequeathed it to later generations as "the way music is supposed to go."

I want to examine here Bach's implementation of Vivaldian tonality in yet another highly conventionalized genre—the binary-form dance. The dance suite developed in France, and Bach's D Major Partita for keyboard is stylistically the most self-consciously French of all his efforts: the opening movement presents an elaborate French overture, the sarabande begins with a flourish of outrageous preciosity, and so on. Yet for all its Versailles trappings, each movement enacts the conversion of French *bon goût* into Italianate dynamism. Bach thus stages a fusion between two ideologically saturated versions of tonality, as the contrast between the stable and dynamic aspects of tonality (which in Vivaldi were divided between group and soloists) here is mapped onto national types. On the one hand, we are given the orderly, rationally constrained procedures of French dance; on the other, we have the desire-driven, individualistic striving of Italian aria and concerto.

It is no coincidence that this fusion was staged by someone identified with neither cultural center. The French—long forbidden contact with the more incendiary Italian style—absorbed elements of it in a most gingerly fashion, even after such interactions were permitted. And although certain aspects of French propriety were imported into the Italian courts, the propulsive drive of Italian musical procedures never suffered much compromise. Unruly passions might have been domesticated by their containment within da capo formats and affective codes, but the end result was the display of turbulence successfully channeled by reason. By contrast, the French rarely tolerated ungrounded energy for more than part of a measure.

Two constructions of the body, founded on very different metaphorical bases, are also at stake here. French music almost always implies the dance, and the rhythmic patterns of the surface are keyed to kinesthetic movements of arms and feet, to regular alternations between motion and the restoration of equilibrium. Within the absolutist régime, French dance served to inscribe the bodies of courtiers into conformity with one another, according to the dictates of a regulating hierarchy. By contrast, Italian music since the madrigal had been concerned with the articulation of interiority—with violent passions, with constructions of impulsive desire and languorous pleasure. The French body performed social dances symbolizing platonic civility; the Italians developed an extensive vocabulary that permitted performers to remain stock-still while dramatizing in sound an inner turmoil that sought to overflow its bounds. Neither version, let me emphasize, is the authentic body—there is no such thing. Both count as socially grounded practices, each located within an ideology of behavioral ideals, each shaping a different experience of reality for those who heard and internalized its patterns.

Since Bach was located in a cultural backwaters, he was relatively free to appropriate whatever musical styles came his way. We know that he fell under the spell of Vivaldi's way of channeling musical energies and that he was an aficionado of the Italian opera performed in Dresden. But in Germany, where every petty court pumped itself up in slavish imitation of Versailles, French dance music acquired great institutional prestige. The nobility and their attendants spoke only

French, disdaining German as a barbaric tongue. Accordingly, some of our most detailed accounts of French performance practices—and even the grouping of dances into the standardized commodity, the suite—come to us from German sources, from those who wanted to be able to replicate authentic French models down to the last detail.

Because music can pass over national boundaries relatively easily and because we no longer have any investment in what these differences might have signified, we often pay little attention to Bach's constructions. But this is not so in literary studies. Court poets in Germany at the time had to master French and write within its codes that spelled the utmost in what was known as *Civilisation*. When in the mid-eighteenth century a number of poets began writing in their despised native language, they sought to challenge *Civilisation* (which restricted its effects to the surface of the body and its behaviors) with what they called *Kultur:* the cultivation and expression of inner resources and feelings that revealed the superiority of the sensitive German bourgeois over the shallow artificiality of the Francophile aristocrat. As Norbert Elias has shown, the rise of *Kultur* produced the beginnings of German nationalist literatures, with Sturm und Drang and Romanticism identifiable as successive waves.[25]

Although Bach wrote dozens of French dances over the course of his career, his adopted Italianate sensibility created an uncomfortable fit, creating precisely the kinds of tensions that exerted an irresistible appeal for him. In many of his dances, it is possible to overlook how these two aspects of his music chafe. But in the D Major Partita, he enacts a collision between the two that resonates strongly with what Elias describes as the subverting of *Civilisation* by the forces of *Kultur*. Thus the opening movement may be a French overture (in the style closely associated with Louis XIV), yet the dotted opening section loses its marchlike quality in a sequence of suspension chains that begin parsing the motion out in three-beat units, and the allegro that follows is nothing other than a Vivaldian concerto for solo harpsichord. Similarly, in the Allemande, a serene beginning gives way to streams of Italianate figuration, devolving into the tortured pathos of interiority.

But it is in Bach's Courante that French platonic order suffers most in the encounter with surging Italianate desire. In keeping with very old practices, the binary form of this dance breaks into two parts, the first of which proceeds to the dominant, the second back to the tonic. The interest in a classic courante derives from its intricate accent patterns: a measure may be grouped in three different ways (into three half-notes, into a whole plus a half, or divided down the middle into two dotted halves), and the dancer in a ballroom would execute different steps, depending on the placement of the accents. This flexibility in harmonic rhythm focuses the attention on the lowest metric level—the ear cannot anticipate what will happen even from measure to measure, let alone at a higher level. Thus if a courante moves from the opening key area to another, it does so with little fanfare or drama. The tonal process serves to ensure rational, platonic order, as theorized by Rameau around that same time.

Bach's Courante accepts the binary-form framework of his models, and he even adopts—at least temporarily in the first few measures—the intricate accent shifts of his French models. But he subtly alters the premises of his models by casting the cadence concluding each half not as a given of structure or harmonic syntax but as a hard-to-win object of desire. The theatrical Vivaldian strategies he employs to build expectations, delays, intensifications, and so on quickly overwhelm the stately measure-to-measure procedure characteristic of the French courante.

As though he intends to follow his French models meticulously, Bach begins his Courante somewhat ambiguously (Ex. 3.4). The opening gesture would seem to come to rest on beat 4, suggesting division of the bar into two equal halves. Yet the melodic ornament on beat 5 tilts the motion forward, even though (and true to convention) equilibrium is reinstated on the following downbeat. The second measure repeats the first, with the materials in the two hands exchanged. But this ambiguity soon begins to seek some kind of continuation other than the dependable resolution onto the downbeat—a resolution that, incidentally, would be necessary if the dancing body were actually to perform

Example 3.4: Bach, D Major Partita for keyboard, Courante: first half

this composition as a courante. Thus the right hand in measure 3 condenses its motive and arrives at its peak a beat earlier than usual, while the bass compensates by moving to G halfway through. The melody divides the bar into three, the harmonic rhythm into halves, and even though consolidation occurs yet again on the following downbeat, the internal jarring within the measures has become quite uneasy.

After the cadence prepared for measure 5 is displaced by a melodic suspension that refuses to cooperate, Bach drops the pretense that this is a refined, courtly dance. Instead, he unleashes the motives that had been harnessed to the regulated alternation of tension and release, and once unleashed, they begin straining forward, with the dominant key area (the key decreed by convention) the probable goal. A running bass enters to propel the motion forward. But when the cadence occurs in measure 9, it reverts back to the tonic. The action stops momentarily: the absence of the bass on the downbeat renders this would-be arrival unbalanced, indicating that D can no longer satisfy the teleological impulse driving the piece.

Dusting itself off and hitting the road again, the melody begins a sequence in measure 9. Yet sequences, even if they spell order within a Vivaldi context, were regarded as highly suspicious by the French: since sequences point forward in time through mega-groupings to a delayed, yet all-the-more desired moment, they draw attention away from the here and now, from the discipline of repeated bodily motions. Not only does Bach's sequence create that kind of long-range yearning, but its accent groupings become irregular with respect to the Courante's meter.

Once again, we approach cadence in the dominant, A major, and Bach continues to make this modulation sound not like obedience to a formula but as a sui generis action requiring great effort and determination. Halfway through measure 11, the melody arrives on G♯, seemingly disappointed and frustrated as a defiant D in the bass prevents the expected resolution. Another sequence toward the dominant ensues, built from the opening motive replicating itself end to end. While the first two units of the sequence acknowledge the downbeat, however, both overshoot the goal, pulling ever upward. By measure 14, the meter is sacrificed to the exigencies of the climax, and the melody cascades downward, heedless of downbeats.

Suddenly, however, it becomes clear that Bach has rearranged the accents so that by means of an elegant hemiola we can touch down on the long-withheld dominant cadence in measure 16 as though nothing could have been easier. But it requires merely taking the repeat to show how far we have traveled in a mere sixteen bars; if Bach caps this half of the dance with the expected move to the dominant, he has implied then resisted that cadence so many times, has escalated the stakes and dammed up so much energy that the arrival, when it comes, seems scarcely commensurate with the efforts involved. The headlong hurtling of that concluding sequence has to revert in a split second to the artificiality of Versailles, something akin to stuffing a rampant genie back into its bottle.

Although Bach obeys the letter of the conventional law by coming to repose on a dominant triad at half-time, he also problematizes that moment: the restless exuberance of *Kultur* that has long delayed the gratification of this modulation abruptly backs off, granting us that guarantee of *Civilisation*'s etiquette. Yet he situates that moment of apparent submission within nearly audible quotation marks. In the strife between formal propriety and impulsive energy, Bach's heart clearly lies with the latter. Bach does not escape social grounding here, however. If he wreaks havoc on the dance, he does so by means of pitting it against another and incongruous set of practices—those he learned from Vivaldi.

This Courante arises from the basic incompatibility of these two worlds and Bach's attempt at forging a coherent relationship: four times over the course of this dance he takes us from the static rigidity of the ancien régime to the impulsive desire for self-generation that stood as the ideal of the emergent German intelligentsia, showing step by step how emancipation feels. He implodes the aristocratic conventions so fetishized by the German upper classes, just as German bourgeois poets were to define themselves in opposition to French *Civilisation*. In other words, Bach participated in the very important early stages of German national culture, where identity was enacted by taking the forms of court by infusing them with a new energy that disdained the strictures demanded by civilized manners. By seizing the cadence for the conclusion of his demonstration, he even suggests that this teleological process of social transformation too can fit under the accommodating umbrella of reason. Indeed, it seems only by virtue of the energy infused from his Italian models that the conventional dominant has been achieved at all. The adhesive of tonality once again patches together two worlds, making the move from the constraints of court to liberation seem simultaneously hard-won and inevitable.

Ironically, perhaps, this binary dance form with its French aristocratic lineage became the stage on which bourgeois musicians of the eighteenth and nineteenth centuries played out their fantasies of self-generation. To be sure, animating the old dance structure with Italianate rhythmic vigor sometimes seemed a bit like new wine in old bottles. Yet in certain respects, it was precisely the resulting tensions that made the sonata the genre of choice during that period, for the emerging middle class manifested in its philosophy and literature the same ambivalence: a desire to fill the shoes of the nobility coupled with scorn for the rigidity of its forms.

As I suggested earlier, Bach's partita already enacts something of that agenda in the 1730s. Fifty years later, the outline of the binary dance still remains, held together most obviously by the tonal trajectory that allows simultaneously for surface flexibility and yet the assurance of a steel-trap rationality underpinning whatever occurs. But whereas Bach contents himself in his Courante with converting one set of energies into another, the focus soon shifts.

A sonata movement's binary process begins not (as in the Bach courante) with a mock-up of the ancien régime, but with a protagonist whose motives and key will organize the piece. To be sure, many a late eighteenth-century symphony opens by conjuring up Versailles in its slow introduction. But the old world thus conjured serves as a prologue, a vestige quickly dispensed with. The main show is how the subject is constructed once it has emerged—not the fact of emergence itself. Over the course of a movement, we witness—as in the contemporaneous Bildungsroman—the narrative formation of an autonomous musical self as it ventures into other terrains, strengthens its innate resources through motivic development, and finally consolidates the secure identity that confirms the viability of the centered subject.

We can observe most of these concerns in Mozart's 1786 "Prague" Symphony, which opens with a slow introduction marked with the dotted rhythms of the French overture. Although the introduction's military rhythms and instruments suggest absolutist power (this is no longer Bach's gallant dancing élite), it begins quite benevolently. But the constant intrusion of sentimental gestures eventually seems to provoke this power into revealing itself in its most oppressive form: it turns suddenly from radiant D major to malignant D minor, and while a pleading violin line seeks to rise, the brass and timpani repeatedly come in to thwart all movement. The introduction closes locked on a dominant pedal from which there appears to be no escape (Ex. 3.5).

In contrast to Bach, Mozart does not show us how the protagonist of the movement's main part manages to pull out of that apparently hopeless situation. After a fermata, the new subject simply takes over—

Example 3.5: Mozart, "Prague" Symphony, Introduction (mm. 1–4; 33–36)

shaky at first, but without a trace of the events that might be posited somewhere in the gap between the fermata and the Allegro. Just as a film might fade on a prison scene, then move directly to a scene we understand to be situated some years later, so Mozart suggests "that was then, this is now." Yet what causes us to accept without much hesitation this fairly abrupt juxtaposition (besides the convention of introductions) is the fact that however much the materials associated with that dominant pedal imply the impossibility of progress, the harmonic function itself stands in a cause/effect relationship with the tonic. Thus when the main part of the movement begins in D major (albeit with a radically different affect), the new materials serve as the proper, even inevitable resolution of the old. No struggle, no Bastille, certainly no Reign of Terror. We just find ourselves relocated in the new order.

The ancien régime does not disappear entirely from Mozart's scenario: its martial forces intrude again quite unexpectedly in the recapitulation of the last movement, only to be outwitted and banished from the scene by the finale's trickster theme. This return of the repressed from the beginning of the symphony makes this piece one of the first to exploit cyclic relationships among movements. But the "Prague" focuses less on how we get to the new order as on what kind of subject will inhabit it. Once past the introduction, the opening movement pursues two agendas—both crucial agendas in most areas of culture at the time: first, the self-generation of the self from relatively unformed beginnings to full maturation, and second, the demonstration that the persona thus fashioning itself also harbors deep inner feelings. Again, the critical distinction in German thought between aristocratic *Civilisation* and bourgeois *Kultur* demands this articulation of inside versus outside, yet it also demands that the seam between the two be rendered invisible—that we come to believe in the inseparability of the two, in the unified consistency of the centered subject.

In the "Prague," Mozart satisfies the external narrative of becoming by starting with an unusually insecure theme that stammers somewhat like Scarlatti's Griselda, that even seems uncertain about which of its elements—melody or bass—constitutes its identity. Eventually, however, it develops into a triumphant closing theme that is every bit as powerful (if nonviolent) as the materials in the militant introduction (Ex. 3.6). As in Vivaldi or Bach, the coherence of this narrative is guaranteed by the tonal trajectory it traces; the evolutionary process from child to hero seems generated through cause/effect relationships. But as though to assure us that the process is not merely one already determined by the conventions of tonal structure, Mozart also weaves a web of motivic correspondences throughout the movement. For although it is to be a universal story he tells, it also must be marked as idiosyncratic. Much later, Schenker sought to explain unity and coherence in this repertory on the basis of standard background progressions, while Rudolph Réti located unity in the tight motivic connections unique to each piece. Although these may seem to represent very different, even mutually exclusive approaches to analysis, the "Prague" insists that both aspects are crucial: Mozart is playing both games. As Terry Eagleton has demonstrated, the same tension between subjective universality and idiosyncrasy shows up repeatedly in aesthetic and political philosophies formulated at the same time. For that moment, anyway, they seemed compatible.[26]

The other agenda—that of incorporating into this otherwise public persona some evidence of the inner self—is managed in two significant spots in the "Prague": most obviously in the slow movement, but also in the articulation of the sonata movement's second key area. In both places, the relentless striving for development and for identity pauses temporarily, and a more lyrical region—marked by the signs of *Empfindsamkeit*, or "sensitivity"—suddenly becomes the center of attention. As Maynard Solomon has pointed out, Mozart often represents with extraordinary precision the darker sides of subjectivity: longings and painful vulnerabilities locked away from public view, scarcely even acknowledged by the individual who bears and nurtures them.[27]

As in the genres from earlier in the eighteenth century, the "Prague" relies on tonality's harmonic flexibility to persuade us that we are hearing individualistic expression and also on its secure linear trajectory to

Example 3.6: Mozart, "Prague," theme 1 beginning/end of exposition (mm. 37–43; 130–36)

ensure coherence. Mozart moves in and out of this moment of interiority in the second theme as though working locks on a canal: the dynamic project of becoming is suspended, making way for a detour into lyricism and even melancholy before pulling back to the principal agenda. Yet the fact that this detour is situated within such a fundamental tonal procedure—the expansion of the dominant key area—permits it to sound natural and unforced: its interruptive quality is papered over.

The brand of centered subjectivity we still cling to, despite its contradictions and discontinuities, finds perhaps its most compelling demonstration in Mozart. He shows us that we can have it all: idiosyncratic characteristics, but with the guarantee of universality; narratives of aggressive self-generation, but with the assurance that one also possesses spiritual depth.[28]

In all the genres discussed in the course of this chapter, tonality effects the reconciliation of certain qualities that might well be understood as incompatible. In Scarlatti's aria we have the control of emotion through reason; in the Vivaldi concerto the mutual interdependence of group and individual; in the Bach courante the explosive infusion of Italian energies into the forms of French court culture; in Mozart's symphony the production of a dynamic self with an immutable, sensitive core. And tonality provides the glue that makes all these fantasies seem to cohere. If conventions could ever be said to have possessed wisdom, these eighteenth-century procedures certainly would be candidates. When we hear the words "Western values" applied to music, they usually refer to this extraordinary period when it was possible to believe unequivocally in such possibilities.

But these models of subjectivity and social interaction did not survive long without serious opposition; indeed, as I have argued elsewhere, many instances of contestation occurred even within the eighteenth century.[29] Like any other human construct, tonality and its structures were arbitrary to a large extent: they were historically mediated, contingent on whatever musical procedures were at hand that could be rechanneled in accordance with new ideals. Examining those processes of rechanneling can give us invaluable insight into the priorities of this period, its music, and its meanings.

But we can also learn a great deal by studying how and why the nineteenth century shifted away from these procedures, when composers such as Beethoven were intent on revealing the artifice, the constructedness—even the flimsiness—of what had been taken as Enlightenment truth. If faith in tonality had not been so palpable, the responses to its various subsequent unmaskings would not have been so traumatic. And that will be the focus of the next chapter.

CHAPTER 4

# The Refuge of
# Counterconvention

In 1992 I attended a bizarre though strangely haunting production of Wagner's *Der fliegende Holländer* by the Minnesota Opera. The final act opened with the chorus of nice Norwegian maidens and sailors singing together as a normal—if extremely conservative—community. When the local sailors invited those from the visiting ship to join in their revelry, the stage suddenly split open to reveal a gaping chasm from which the demonic crew (made up to resemble refugees from *Night of the Living Dead*) sang their responses. After that horrendous moment, the stage remained ruptured, incapable of being restored to its original condition. The subsequent scene between Senta and Erik took place around the edges of that chasm.

Near the end of the opera, after the Dutchman had made his stormy exit, Senta rushed to the back of the stage to a catwalk that extended against the back wall. As she sang her final lines, a door in front of which she stood opened, and the ghoulish Dutchman stepped forth. With the concluding bars of the opera, their catwalk suddenly hurtled forward over the abyss to the front of the stage; Senta's community watched on in horror as these two monstrous yet magnificently autonomous creatures clung to each other while hovering over the yawning pit below. And the rapturous closing music told us that this is the fate to which we should aspire: to break away from the conformity of social bonds and to launch off into the ecstasy of the void.

More than anything I have experienced recently, director Keith Warner's staging of *Dutchman* made me reflect on the grotesqueness but also on the undeniable appeal of Romantic alienation. Whether the opera ends in the traditional manner with Senta leaping to her death, thereby redeeming her undead *Übermensch*, or with Minnesota Opera's staged allegory of self-imposed exile, Wagner's finale gives us what we are meant to take as a happy ending. Not a happy ending, to be sure, in the eyes of any of the dumbstruck Norwegians gawking from the sidelines; yet happy to those of us who share with Wagner and his lead characters their longing to free themselves of the social world with all its rules, its compromises, its inability to appreciate true inner worth. Under the influence of Wagner's glorious strains, who could resist identifying with his misunderstood elect?

With *Der fliegende Holländer*, we seem to have come a very long way from the consensus models that secured a rational basis for eighteenth-century culture. Vivaldi's marvelous vision of productive collaboration between virtuosic individuals and the social group for the sake of shared progress has mutated into this scenario that pits valiant, idealistic (if somewhat pathological) selves against a small-minded, uncomprehending mob. Nor is it simply the opera plots and song lyrics of the nineteenth century that manifest this ideological shift but also the increasing distrust of the musical procedures that had allowed eighteenth-century constructions to appear natural—foremost among these, tonality and its forms.

Now, there is no objective reason why the inherited musical language itself had to have been targeted as the enemy. As we saw in our examination of eighteenth-century tonality in chapter 3, this convention was flexible enough to underwrite any number of scenarios while still ensuring intelligibility. And during the nineteenth century, composers in Italy, France, and elsewhere—many of them deeply committed to progressive political agendas—continued happily to utilize this and other conventions in order to maximize communication and social impact. But in German-speaking regions, the musical lingua franca itself was cast as part of the problem.[1] By the end of the nineteenth century, tonality—that guarantor of reason and shared ideals—had been declared bankrupt. Not because of attacks from the outside by barbarian hordes but because this fantasy of retreat—retreat from society, retreat even from the discursive practices that allow society to cohere— had itself become the overriding convention within High Art. Like Senta, stylistically advanced German music split itself off irrevocably from community in accordance with Romantic notions of individualistic expression.

Why did this happen? Why particularly in Germany? These are difficult questions, and answering them has been impeded by the myth that German music did, in fact and as the result of "natural" emancipatory impulses, transcend social influences to take up residence in the realm of the "purely musical."[2] This myth is so powerful that its own self-justifications have largely been accepted and have prevailed as truth. Only recently have historians begun to examine German Romanticism in terms other than those established by its first apologists, to uncover the kinds of cultural conventions that permitted this self-proclaimed antisocial movement to make social sense.

Several factors helped to create this logic of retreat into the refuge of counterconvention. As was mentioned in the last chapter, Norbert Elias has explained how eighteenth-century German culture constituted itself in part as a reaction against what was perceived as the superficiality of Francophile courts.[3] In contrast to the *Civilisation* of absolutist society and its rule-bound artifacts, German *Kultur* sought the unmediated expression of the inner self. But a whiff of pathology clung to this notion of the inner self, right from the outset. Klaus Doerner, in his study of attitudes toward insanity in various parts of modern Europe, has argued that only in Germany was genius defined in ways that often made it indistinguishable from dementia. When the public signs of reason came to be regarded as impediments to free self-development, then the (no less public) signs of irrationality became a popular alternative. He explains that in Germany

> Liberal capitalism and its economic crises were accompanied by waves of Romanticism, a testimony to the fact Romanticism was no match for rational social reality. The antirational realities were as much an expression of social refusal as of escapist movements, as much a realistic protest against all rational constriction of bourgeois existence as an irrational cul-de-sac. That held true for the evolutionary development of history, for the myth of the *Volk*, and for emanational logic, as well as for the romanticization of the sinister-mysterious, the imaginary and unconscious, the dreams and utopian wish-fulfillments, of wandering, solitude, and homelessness, of childhood and fairytales, of strangeness and estrangement, of moods and drives, of physical and mental disease.[4]

This fetishizing of the signs of morbid sensibility began to make themselves manifest in music in the staged eccentricities of C. P. E. Bach's fantasias. Moreover, the particular fixations Doerner lists have obvious correlations in the Romantic repertory—not only wanderers, fairytales, and moods of stories like *The Flying Dutchman*, but also the emphasis on an oddly nonsocial, evolution-based history (witness Forkel's biography of J. S. Bach or E. T .A. Hoffmann's discussion of the Viennese classicists)[5] and on the belief in a logic that does not emerge from human conventions but emanates from on high—or (what may be the same thing) from "the music itself."

Friedrich Kittler's *Discourse Networks, 1800/1900* makes even clearer what was at stake in this set of refusals. German artists belonged to a society in which the bourgeois class had attained only a very tentative toehold by the late eighteenth century. Unlike their counterparts in France and England, both of which had well-established traditions of middle-class intellectuals who participated actively in public forums, in which consensus politics were rather more viable, the emergent German intelligentsia had little access to the arenas where policy was determined;

more often than not, artists and their audiences worked as civil-service bureaucrats whose mental efforts were quickly absorbed into the system without a trace. Art became, then, a compensatory sphere where alienated members of this white-collar labor force could assure themselves of their uniqueness, their deep personal feelings.[6]

But as Kittler's term "discourse networks" implies, the autonomy of this compensatory sphere was more illusory than real. For although these artists had succeeded in breaking free from the patronage of courts and church, they found themselves dependent on a market economy; they were forced to cultivate a clientele for the literary and musical works they produced. An enormous amount of cultural energy had to be exerted to convince artist and consumer alike that the experience transacted by means of publishers and distributors was, in fact, unmediated. Although connoisseurs could not avoid recognizing some of this multilayered mediation, they increasingly sought to divide those public aspects of the work that would seem to make it commodifiable from those—perceptible only to themselves—that maintained artistic integrity, despite market intervention.[7]

In poetry, two socially conditioned modes of reception emerged, both with gendered implications. Women, who actually constituted the largest segment of the poetry-reading public, were encouraged to relate sentimentally to its manifest content, to believe that what they read faithfully represented the poet's very soul. By contrast, male readers, while also presumably responding to that content, worked to maintain a disinterested stance as they concentrated on unraveling the formal and hermeneutic intricacies of what they read; they assured themselves that the true substance of the work resided there in the structure and intricate web of cultural references—not on the surface that was available even to the casual female reader.

A similar pattern developed in music, as composers found that the most reliable markets were those that catered to the domestic scene. Increasingly, they found themselves responding to publishers' requests for the short piano pieces, songs, and arrangements that could be managed by amateur performers, who demanded large quantities of such music. Even the genres of symphony and opera had to satisfy entrepreneurs who sought to attract an untutored audience, which reacted most enthusiastically to dramatic, rhetorically vivid compositions—an audience that in terms of its powers of discrimination might as well have been made up wholly of women.

Consequently, those who prided themselves on their authentic understanding of Romantic music tended to denigrate the tastes and listening habits of the audiences and women who made up such a large portion of the music-consuming public.[8] This gendered division still remains. In his book *Nineteenth-Century Music*, Carl Dahlhaus argues that even the greatest art can be transformed into *Kitsch* if played by and for women.[9] And one of the tasks critics such as E. T. A. Hoffmann, Schumann, and Hanslick took upon themselves was the production of a new kind of consumer: one who would renounce the easy pleasures of sentimentality or virtuosity and gravitate toward music that rewarded what Adorno later would call structural listening.[10] Kittler calls this critical enterprise the "reception industry"—the instilling of "proper" habits of listening or reading, which focus on formal matters rather than banal manifest content.

Steven Rumph has argued compellingly that Hoffmann's celebrated account of Beethoven's Fifth Symphony ignores the rhetorical, dramatic, melodic, and coloristic aspects of the piece and concentrates instead on harmonic relations—the implied locus of the symphony's "true meaning."[11] This critical approach, which purports to have moved beyond mere representation to deal with "the music itself" (in Hoffmann's theologically charged language, "a kingdom not of this world"), was originally tied to the political bid of German *Kultur* for moral superiority; as Rumph states, "[b]ehind Hoffmann's ethereal *Geisterreich* lurks the sordid violence of the all-too-real kingdoms of this world."[12] In other words, even this bid for autonomy is inextricably linked to social crises. Moreover, the resulting ideology, which developed from Prussian attempts at securing cultural identity in the wake of Napoleon, still governs our educational practices.[13] Yet if it might be argued that artists and critics often privileged these technical levels, it was still the "compromised" level of tonal narrative, affect, and dramatic gesture that influenced the lives of those who listened, that actually performed most of the cultural work, that determined which music survived and which disappeared from the repertory.

Composers did not reject conventions simply because they were conventions, however; they also reacted against the cultural uses made of such codes during their eighteenth-century heyday. Recall briefly the examples discussed in chapter 3. If Scarlatti's *Griselda* displayed supreme confidence in the fidelity of its mimetic codes, subsequent generations heard those patterns as cardboard cut-outs. From a later vantage point, much of what had appeared so powerful in Scarlatti's formulas became intolerably artificial, precipitating a deep distrust in such codes of representation. Eighteenth-century style boasted the ability to "capture" and rationalize affect, but in the process it essentialized a particular kind of reason and excluded a whole range of human experiences.

For the rational strictures of *opera seria* were shaped in part by the desire of the nobility to exercise control over behaviors, to regulate ethics, subjectivity, gender, and class relations. Thus if Griselda gets to be the heroine of this opera, it is so that she can exhibit her utter selflessness. She exercises her rationality *not* in order to establish her individuality but the better to serve her monarch. If she, a commoner, finally gets to mount the throne, it is so that the king can reveal his benevolence, his responsiveness to true merit. Recall also that a class riot opened the first act of Scarlatti's *Griselda*, as the People insisted on the unworthiness of the king's low-born consort; but the opera proves that the People were wrong, that the king alone knows what is best. Such structures of belief were not likely to provoke enthusiastic responses from audiences a hundred years later, even if Scarlatti and Zeno intended them as manifestations of "universal reason."[14]

Similarly, Vivaldi's concerto model enacted the compatibility of social group and self. But it did not take long for that script to be called into question, rewritten so that potential tensions in the model became discernible. I have written elsewhere about Bach's Fifth Brandenburg, in which a rebellious harpsichord solo comes close to wrecking the collaborative process so crucial to Vivaldi, and also about the slow movement of Mozart's Piano Concerto K. 453, in which consensus appears to be achieved through coercion.[15]

Further, if Bach's Courante enacts the successful emergence of free libidinal energy from oppressive conformity, this plot archetype turns out to be quite ambivalent with respect to another important aspect of Enlightenment ideology: namely, discursive consensus. For the heroic narrative of bursting open the conventional dimensions of an inherited style became itself a dominant convention of the nineteenth century. And once this modernist scenario of violent oedipal usurpations took hold, each liberatory style became the oppressive tradition from which the succeeding one had to break loose. Style overthrew style with the regularity of banana-republic coups, leading to a historical trajectory that virtually guaranteed (as self-fulfilling prophecy) the dissolution of the premises that make communication feasible.

As Brandenburg No. 5 or K. 453 make clear, such revolutionary impulses risk unleashing—even self-consciously exploiting—the irrational. Both pieces so favor the yearnings of the idiosyncratic individual that they call community into question—though if Bach and Mozart attenuate social contract, they conclude their pieces by attesting to its necessity. As subjective freedom verges on madness in the flight from convention, eighteenth-century composers show us how socially sanctioned norms save us from ourselves. Yet to imagine alternative endings for either Bach or Mozart is to foresee what actually happened over the course of the century that culminated finally in the emergence of atonality. Both Bach and Mozart opted for negotiated settlements with social norms in their bids for closure. But in the nineteenth century, appeals to community exerted less and less influence on artists or on the ideal listeners who learned to cheer stylistic transgressions from the sidelines. Norms become the enemy.

Finally, if Mozart's "Prague" granted the illusion of rational continuity between public exteriors and inner depth, this too came to be doubted. The laminated components came apart, and portrayals of internal integrity required increasingly erratic surfaces and the refusal of shared expectations. Again, it is important to remember that this crisis occurred primarily in Germany, where it was only in the terrain of the imagination that these kinds of narratives could be enacted. If we take the autonomous bourgeois subject to be what is at stake in these musical procedures (again, this need not have happened—it didn't in most parts of contemporaneous Europe), then reified elements such as codes, normative procedures, and modes of representation had to be discarded—or at least disavowed.

But once this convention of skepticism developed, it came to dominate much of Western aesthetic thought, and it still prevails—even in domains not yet imagined in nineteenth-century Germany. For instance, jazz and rock, both of which developed within highly contested social contexts,[16] are now often regarded as having developed sophistication only when their practitioners revolted against the pressures exerted by the means of communication themselves. In order to escape what is regarded as the feminized world of pop reception, jazz retreated—or advanced—into the realm of free jazz, rock into art rock, punk, and so-called alternative.

If the contradictions in music's enactments of Enlightenment reason can be glimpsed even in affirmative examples, they became ever more pronounced as the eighteenth century approached its end. We might well celebrate Griselda's ability to pull conflicting emotions under one tonal umbrella, Vivaldi's to enact collaboration between community and individual, Bach's to perform rebellion without bloodshed, or Mozart's to reveal the integrity of centered subjectivity—all effects of tonality. But what does it mean when, in the opening scene of *Don Giovanni*, a single tonal trajectory embraces a servant's complaints about class privilege, a rape, a duel, and a murder? Without question, we have to admire Mozart's virtuosity in accomplishing such a feat. Yet what kind of reason is it that naturalizes this violent sequence by means of form? Is it "Fate"? Or a cynical display of instrumental reason of the sort favored by Mozart's contemporary, the Marquis de Sade?

For the aesthetic perfection of eighteenth-century music is often an effect of the composer's ability to manipulate tonal form; and to the extent that we relegate this effect to domains of technique or platonic order, we overlook the ways in which such conventions perform cultural work. Whereas tonality had been an operative signifying device in all the other examples we have discussed, in this opening scene of *Don Giovanni* it positions itself as "purely musical," thus bestowing a metaphysical seal of approval on whatever proceedings it embraces. In appearing to have transcended meaning, these conventions elevated to the status of the "purely musical" signify utterly.

I have undertaken this critique of eighteenth-century practices not because I wish to denigrate their principles—indeed, my allegiances lie closest to that moment in music history when the premises of the musical language were sufficiently shared to permit genuine public exchange—but because I want to present a reasonably sympathetic account of why and how this world came to be rejected. One of the overriding conventions of the eighteenth century was reconciliation. But once that ideal was called into doubt, then this whole set of carefully balanced cultural fantasies began to collapse.

It was precisely because tonality and its forms had seemed to demonstrate the viability of a post-theological world—a world promising perfect integrity on virtually every level without divine intervention—that its dissolution proved so devastating. Negotiation and communication had started to be distrusted already by the early nineteenth century, just when emerging social conditions seemed to demand such activities more urgently than at any previous moment in European history. Feelings were now thought to resist expression through shared devices; individual artists associated social agreement with loss of autonomy; and signs of the true "organic" art came to be buried deep beneath the rhetorical surfaces demanded by audiences.

Yet this crisis of secular faith bequeathed to us some of the most extraordinary cultural documents we possess. I will spend most of the rest of this chapter dealing with Beethoven's String Quartet in A Minor, Op. 132, for several reasons. First, because I want to demonstrate that (contrary to popular belief) I can say something nice about Beethoven.[17] Second, because Op. 132 so clearly enacts the tension between, on the one hand, a loss of belief in the very conventions upon which Beethoven himself had earlier relied and, on the other, the desire to speak despite obvious skepticism that speech is possible. And finally, because of an exquisite article Joseph Kerman wrote for *The Hudson Review* early in his career in which he attempted to account for the public, narrative dimensions of this quartet.[18] As an homage to Joe, who invited me to deliver the lectures on which this book is based, I want to translate his reading into my somewhat different terms. I will also incorporate along the way some of the insights of Kofi Agawu, who has published a discussion of the background structure in the quartet's first movement,[19] and I will be proposing a kind of reconciliation between Kerman's humanist interpretation and Agawu's formal analysis. As always, my view of Beethoven and his place in music history owes a great deal to the framework established by Adorno and explicated so compellingly by Rose Subotnik.[20]

Few pieces offer so vivid an image of shattered subjectivity as the opening page of Op. 132 (Ex. 4.1). In contrast to typical sonata movements, which pursue the activities of a principal theme, this one presents within its first key area four radically contrasting ideas, differentiated not only by melodic contour but by the worlds to which they would seem to refer—if, indeed, reference can be said to be operative any longer. Agawu reads the exposition as a random assortment of *topoi*

Example 4.1: Beethoven, Op. 132, movement 1 (mm. 1–22)

littering the surface; and although he carefully classifies them all according to traditional associations, he decides ultimately that they do not signify anything coherent. Consequently, he dives below the wreckage of the surface in hopes of discovering continuity at a deeper level.

By contrast, Kerman prefers to interpret the surface as signifying, even if the process he traces borders on incoherence. For it surely cannot be coincidental that the tattered signifiers that parade by in confusion in this movement refer to the most readily recognized, the most privileged of genre-types. In order, they conjure up the Renaissance motet, the virtuoso solo cadenza/recitative, the pathos-ridden aria, and the march; the transition adds a dance. Moreover, the affective devices embedded in all these snippets draw on a long history of shared codes: the twisting minor seconds, yearning sevenths, ambiguous diminished chords, distorted Neapolitan inflections, appoggiaturas, and suspensions that make up the surface all belong to the most agonized corner of an affective palette that descends from the Renaissance madrigal. What emerges from this collage of deracinated, apparently unrelated *topoi* is at least a consistent tone described by Kerman as "suffering." We may not be able to make immediate sense of the succession of events in Op. 132, but we can at least recognize the signs of anguish.

In other words, if Beethoven does everything within his power to shred conventions as he goes, he can proceed only by means of those very conventions. He calls up moments of an orderly social world, with its religious rituals, dances, military exercises, lyric songs, and modes of virtuosic display, even though his collage destabilizes their meanings. We may be witnessing the rantings of a madman who has lost the ability to forge articulate meanings, or a nightmare in which warped fragments of the everyday appear as though randomly shuffled, or a level of interiority that refuses to marshall its impulses into the tidy wrappers of eighteenth-century form. As Petrarch wrote following Laura's death, "i miei gravi sospir non vano in rime, il mio duro martir vince ogni stile" (my deep sighs will not submit to rhyme, my harsh martyrdom defeats all styles).[21] Yet neither Beethoven nor Petrarch could, in fact, escape language, kick against it though they might—and thus the frustration Kerman hears as the overriding emotion of the movement. Nowhere in this quartet do we find unmediated expression.

Structural unfolding often serves as the key to inchoate openings, especially during this period when the act of "becoming" figures so prominently in cultural agendas. Recall that the *Eroica* begins with little more than a snippet, which gradually earns a sustainable identity by means of annexing whatever it encounters; even the law-abiding eighteenth-century pieces examined in chapter 3 involve the eventual reconciliation between heterogeneous elements. We might anticipate, therefore, that the conflicted beginning of Op. 132 will have achieved coherent articulation by the end of the movement. And indeed, the exposition's second theme not only presents a balanced instance of what seems a full-fledged entity (Ex. 4.2) but proceeds to start annexing into its affirmative context the snippets from the opening section: the erratic sixteenth notes of what Kerman calls a scream become the means for directed forward motion, the march rhythms lend decisiveness, and the tortured intervals of the motet now contribute only the signs of yearning that the sensitive bourgeois subject must possess. Yet at the last moment of the exposition, the fusion falls apart.

Note that the attempted synthesis takes place in F major, the sixth degree that increasingly stands for Never Never Land in the economy of nineteenth-century musical imagery.[22] In later Beethoven and, especially, Schubert, the submediant often substitutes for the too-conventional, too-rational dominant as the second key area. As a major-key area within a minor-key hierarchy, it variously radiates hope, escape, or nostalgia for a lost arcadia—indeed, it comes to invoke a sense of longing for the arcadia of the Enlightenment, even though the irrationality of such devices marks them as irrevocably alienated from the Edenic world of the previous generation. But it takes only a half-step drop in the bass to return the piece to harsh, unmerciful reality—which is what happens here at the end of Beethoven's exposition. Hope is here unmasked as false consciousness.

An abortive development section follows—for what can be developed when we don't even know what the protagonist is? After two brief attempts at linear processing explode, the movement plunges into the extensive formal block that has caused much consternation among analysts. Because it rehearses the principal events of the opening section, it is often labeled a recapitulation—in fact, the first of two, because this very same sequence occurs yet again. Others view it as part of the development because it inhabits the wrong keys: E minor/C major, the first of which consents to the conventional dominant the exposition

Example 4.2: Beethoven, Op. 132, movement 1, second theme (mm. 48–52)

avoided, only to end up in the submediant of that key, threatening a mechanically produced infinite regress. Only the second run-through follows the imperative of returning to tonic, even though in the absence of any clear achievement along the way the triumph of tonic rings hollow. Kerman's early essay treated the two blocks respectively as recapitulation and coda, though in his book on the Beethoven quartets he endorsed the dual-recapitulation solution.

It is, of course, both and neither of these options. What is important is that process itself has been thrown into confusion and thus hovers somewhere between refusing conventional structure altogether and obeying it so mechanically that the reiteration of reified formal blocks threatens to take precedence over the actual materials. I prefer to think of the movement as composed of three attempted expositions, each of which is discarded in preparation for the next. Kerman elsewhere used the image of a table of contents to describe the enigmatic beginning of the Great Fugue,[23] and the first movement of Op. 132 can be heard as three rough drafts of such a table. Fragments of all the materials that will be explored over the course of the whole quartet appear in this opening movement; part of its purpose seems to be to toss into the ring elements that will be assembled or clarified (if at all) only later, beyond the scope of the movement's borders. Yet Beethoven does put these elements through the paces of sonata, as though this scrap heap itself constituted a traditional subject. And despite the radical dismemberment of the opening motto in the coda (each pitch appears in mm. 232–35 in a different instrument as a background pedal tone), he even presents us with "closure" of a sort: a rhythmically decisive cadence on the tonic, A minor, but with a fit of newly spawned violin figuration that seems designed as a means of insisting (however irrationally) that this is the end, goddamn it (Ex. 4.3)!

We are verging on the terrain Fredric Jameson theorizes as the schizophrenic postmodern subject, in which the surface that used to be guaranteed by a sense of underlying depth has become mere surface for the inconsequential playing with signs—the title, in fact, of Agawu's book. John Cage is a crucial figure for Jameson's argument, in that Cage retains external form but fills it with whatever his chance operations happen to yield. In fact, we might imagine a piece by Cage that would produce something like the first page of Op. 132 through the random switching of a radio dial. Yet surely Beethoven—even Beethoven *in extremis*—is not Cage. Kerman answers this dilemma by arguing that Beethoven's ruptured surface produces a carefully calculated effect and by turning to the remainder of the quartet for explication. He trusts that Beethoven is employing those particular signs and procedures for reasons that will eventually become intelligible. Now we see through a glass darkly, then face to face. . . .

Agawu's Schenkerian solution takes a very different tack. What he discovers through his graphing is that "a familiar construct—the circle of fifths—may be shown to underlie the harmonic process of the entire movement, cutting across the obvious points of formal articulation and lending the whole process a subsurface continuity."[24] To be sure, Agawu finds irregularities even in the subsurface (none of his cycles of fifths, for instance, is complete, nor was the circle of fifths ever a dependable guardian of tonal security);[25] yet the relative coherence of this level compensates for the radical discontinuity of the surface. In other

Example 4.3: Beethoven, Op. 132, movement 1, conclusion

words, although "the signifying function of topics is seriously questioned in this movement," meaning has gone underground, where it continues to guarantee subjective integrity.[26] Unlike the eighteenth-century pieces examined in chapter 3, in Op. 132 surface signifiers and depth no longer pretend to stand in a causal relationship with one another—this subcutaneous layer of continuity refuses even to acknowledge the formal divisions of the sonata-esque structure imposed over it. As the public surface becomes a red herring, the concealed private network takes full responsibility for whatever sense the movement makes.

I concur with many of Agawu's conclusions, so long as we remain (as he does) within the opening movement of the quartet. For all my notorious bad-mouthing of Schenkerian methods, I even believe that what Agawu traces here really exists and that it is a crucial aspect of what Beethoven and many others were doing at the time. Indeed, the more detached surface and background became in nineteenth-century music, the more imperative became this underground network. My only objection to Schenkerian accounts is that they are often framed as revealing some kind of bedrock, whereas I would see those intricate connections between middle- and backgrounds as part of the representational apparatus for producing the images of organic subjectivity so fundamental to German Romanticism. And although there seems to be no easy *détente* within the quartet between private inside and public surface, it is this particular set of estrangements that most characterized this moment in cultural history, as analyzed by Elias, Doerner, Kittler, and Rumph.

Put differently: even the stark idiosyncrasies of this movement are embedded within a social context. The crisis Beethoven here traces with such force and internal integrity resonates with a much larger ideological crisis. To say this is not to reduce the details of this quartet to sociology or to imply some kind of determinism, whereby artists passively reflect the conditions within which they live. Jacques Attali has argued that music "prophesies" in the sense that its relative immateriality allows it to fan through the possibilities available within a given model far more quickly than any other medium,[27] and Adorno—with late Beethoven as his principal evidence—demonstrated how serious composers push up and wage war against the social contradictions embedded in their inherited structures. In Op. 132 Beethoven stages a process whereby once-meaningful sonata procedure now usurps and channels—as though by automatic pilot or force—even the most violent attempts at resistance.

To return to Kerman's more hermeneutic account: Beethoven designs this opening in such a way as to deflect forward the listener's desire to witness the consolidation of meaning, away from the typically autonomous first movement and toward the series of movements that follows. And here we find each of the associative shards introduced in the first section now expanded into a full-blown articulation: first, the dance and affirmative lyrical elements, then the sacred motet with the *Heiliger Dankgesang*, next a march interrupted by recitative, and at last a finale marked with the singing pathos of the fragment that emerged as the anchor of movement 1 (Ex. 4.4).

If the topoi of the introduction seemed an arbitrary assortment, like shuffled tarot cards, they begin to become meaningful when each becomes a whole episode arranged within a linear sequence; at the very least it becomes clear that their traditional associations are intended. Along with Kerman, I hear this sequence as representing something of a journey—though emphatically not the always-already guaranteed journey to Utopia of the standard tonal process, best exemplified by Beethoven's own middle period. If there is heroicism in Op. 132, it manifests itself not in the triumph of identity (the story sonata and tonality tend to tell, left to their own devices), but in the fact that its implied persona embraces each of its topical realms in turn, finds that no single one provides a satisfactory answer, and eventually attempts to forge an ending even though closure itself—along with unconflicted identity—has been acknowledged as vanity. If the subject of Op. 132 is not the unified tune of the *Eroica* but rather that tangle of contradictory impulses revealed on the opening page, then this process is perhaps an ideal way of telling its story while preserving its peculiar form of identity. To reconcile the antinomies would be to destroy what is fundamental to this particular subject.

The journey's trajectory begins in movement 2 with an excursion into the social world of dance. In contrast to the still-unhealed fissures of the opening, this second movement insists on motivic homogeneity. The movement's persona clutches at unity but to such a degree that hampers its potential for dynamic development, despite the contrapuntal intricacies that lead Kerman to compare it to a highly polished jewel. And even this motivic rigor fails to keep at bay the anxieties left

Example 4.4: Beethoven, Op. 132, beginnings of movements 2 through 5

over from the first movement: the trio turns alternately trivial with its whining musette and terrifying with its unprepared eruptions of violence. By consolidating identity this rigidly, the movement has no way of responding to or reconciling itself with other elements.

The *Heiliger Dankgesang* takes us again into that fantasy world of the submediant, now endowed through its lydian flavor and motet-like materials with the signs of an archaic religiosity so cherished by the early Romantics. While we are surely to believe on some level in the faith proffered in this movement, its placement in the middle of the quartet and on F mark it as something other than a rational goal: this experience of the sublime may make continuation possible, but it cannot stand as the Elysium toward which the trajectory strives.

The causality taken for granted in earlier tonal compositions gives way in the oblique shifts between the F lydian *Dankgesang* and the passages in D major designated in the score as *Neue Kraft füllend*. It is in retrospect that the dominant-tonic relationships of the eighteenth century can be heard as implying cause/effect: when they disappear, one realizes the extent to which they cemented together that earlier world, making its various fusions sound natural. If the *Dankgesang* were to proceed to *neue Kraft* through a dominant, the progression would indicate that prayer had in fact resulted in recovery, whereas the oblique pivots in this movement mark the relationship as outside the realm of human reason and agency. This lydian world is framed as ineffable, as mysteriously transcending codes and conventions. Yet even here Beethoven proceeds by recontextualizing and extending the codes available to him.

The march in movement 4 returns us to tonic major, to a clearly social referential context, to secure (even rigid) ego boundaries—but its confidence is absurdly out of keeping with the alternately anxiety-ridden and mystical process that brought us to this point. A kind of narrative sweep that had been perhaps only latent in the tableaux of movements 2 and 3 suddenly takes over. A recitative breaks in, calling the march's lie and breaking open into an expressivity that strains as though toward speech.

And we arrive at the final movement that enacts the dynamic process of sonata-rondo, that accepts the pathos-ridden fragment of the opening page and gives it full rein to lament the loss of wholeness displayed over the course of the quartet. Yet Beethoven does not permit us to find solace even in tragic resignation. At the end of the movement, a sleight-of-hand pulls us abruptly into the major mode for an incongruous happy ending—one no less ironic, though far more devastating, than the one affixed a hundred years later to the conclusion of *Threepenny Opera*.

If this journey through successive aspects of subjectivity fails to produce the apparently airtight trajectory and eventual resolution of the "Prague" Symphony or the *Eroica*, it is in large part because such constructions had lost cultural credibility. The subject for Beethoven in his last years was precisely this process that hovers without choosing among the illusion of unity, the lure of blind faith, the potential of disciplined force, the expression of alienated self-pity, and a hope against hope that makes continuation possible—or that at least provides the impetus for stringing these elements together into a tenuous narrative sequence.

Leo Treitler has written eloquently on the ways Beethoven simultaneously engaged and liquidated his semiotic codes in the finale of the Ninth Symphony.[28] If the composer spends an enormous amount of energy liquidating codes in Op. 132 (and in the Ninth), he spends just as much reinvesting in them, shoring them up against the skepticism with which he himself assails them. As Nietzsche stated much later: "We have to cease to think if we refuse to do it in the prison-house of language." And on the levels of both Agawu's hidden subsurface and Kerman's narrative journey, Beethoven is signifying as though his very life depended on it.

It is already clear in late Beethoven that the center established by eighteenth-century cultural forms would not hold, as the very devices that had appeared to resolve tensions so naturally came to be seen as artificial mediations at best, lies at worst. For the remainder of the century, artists returned again and again to the Enlightenment vision of intersubjective wholeness to try to make it work. Yet the gap between outside and inside, between the possibility of social agreement and desire for un-mediated individuality grew ever wider.

Or at least it did in Germany. Most other European cultures did not adopt this metaphor that reads the autonomous movement or cycle as a performance of self-contained and self-generating subjectivity: operas representing social interactions and multiple points of view continued to flourish in France and Italy, while songs and dance forms retained confidence in verbal language and in collective modes of entertain-ment. Yet if this identification of the piece of music with the radically autonomous individual had not taken root, our narratives about who was important in music history, our analytical methods, and even much of the music produced would be profoundly different.

The ascent of autonomous instrumental music was no simple matter, as the flurry of intellectual activity from aestheticians and music critics indicates. Literary theorist Ross Chambers has pointed out that the move from "readerly" genres that happily embrace convention to "writerly" enterprises that ostensibly cast off convention itself requires submission to stringent higher-level conventions.[29] Thus the need for consensus or social contract did not truly disappear in the nineteenth century, not even in Germany; it was reconstituted as counterconvention, and people had to be taught to appreciate it—thus Kittler's "reception industry."

Beneath the surface—whether discontinuous or deceptively accessi-ble—lay the increasingly more distilled integrity of the "real" subject, available only to those with higher powers of discernment. Peter Mid-dleton has labeled this obsession with hidden subjectivity in Romantic and Modernist culture as "the inner gaze," and he notes that it is usually regarded as a formal issue rather than a concern with a particular ver-sion of the self.[30] In music it was Schenker who discovered how to de-tect that all-important subtext on a systematic basis: if a coherent subject underpinned a movement, Schenker could track its progress; if it did not, he would not hesitate to relegate the piece to the rubbish heap.

The surfaces themselves, however, with their affective qualities and narratives, continued to signify to audiences. And the public dimensions of nineteenth-century music (often ignored or dismissed by today's music specialists) trace the kinds of stories that circulated through other domains of culture: stories that involve vulnerability, violence, anxiety, gender politics, pleasure, exoticism—in other words, the principal issues of the time. To be sure, the manifest content of these pieces is sometimes less comforting than the securely integrated graphs and structures ferreted out by analysts: from certain points of view, Agawu's account of Op. 132 is a good deal less disturbing than Kerman's or mine. But we need to take seriously both public narratives *and* enactments of internal integrity if we are to come to terms with the cultural work performed by "absolute" music rather than trust that the "real" meaning is located in that subterranean network.

The turn into the twentieth century, of course, brought with it another, even more severe crisis over subjectivity. This time, as Kittler has demonstrated at length, it was those few threads that still connected inside integrity with a minimal level of public intelligibility that were assaulted. In order to break entirely free of discourse, which was seen as hopelessly compromised by its associations with a bureaucratized, commodified world, many German writers studied and imitated the utterances of psychiatric patients (some even experimented with the serialization of phonemes in an attempt at liberating language from sense); Schoenberg too drew on images of madness as means of severing all those tenuous links with conventional communication. Artists developed a kind of deliberate autism in order to maintain at all cost that image of the uncontaminated self that had become the only acceptable stance.

As Hal Foster has argued, however, even expressionism constitutes a convention-based language:

> The expressionist quest for immediacy is taken up in the belief that there exists a content beyond convention, a reality beyond representation. . . . [E]xpressionism denies its own status as a language—a denial that is necessary given its claim to immediacy and stress on the self as originary. For with a denial of its rhetorical nature goes a

denial of the mediations that threaten the primacy of individual expression, mediations which are usually dismissed as mere conventions, as cultural not natural. . . . [Expressionism] speaks a language, but a language so obvious we may forget its conventionality and must inquire again how it encodes the natural and simulates the immediate. . . . After all, formlessness does not dissolve convention or suspend mediation; as the expressionist trope for feeling, it is a rhetorical form too. . . . The expressionist monologue, then, is a form of address, one that suppresses its rhetorical nature, it is true, but a form, a formula nonetheless.[31]

No less coded than tonality, the dissonances and discontinuities of atonal music themselves constitute a conventional vocabulary, one derived ultimately from a condensation of traditional signs of madness, rage, suffering.[32] Moreover, beneath these surfaces that seem to attest to radical decentering, the serialists found a way of ensuring the continued presence of centered subjectivity. In pieces by Schoenberg, Boulez, or Babbitt, we know (because we are told, because we know how to analyze scores) that an idiosyncratic but rigorously integrated subject controls the events, however incoherent they may sound. Thus the urgency of set theory and analysis.

To the ear the works of John Cage may not sound all that different from those rigorously ordered by means of combinatorial sets. Yet this is precisely why Cage posed such a threat, for he presented the possibility that beneath that discontinuous surface there lurks . . . nothing at all.[33] The container that had held the subject (even if we only knew that on faith) was now demonstrated to have no walls; moreover, its uncanny resemblance to those vessels we had taken to have depth also called them retrospectively into question.

With the voiding out of that particular generative metaphor, we reach the end of a cultural trajectory. It is not, to be sure, a trajectory that many have cared about recently—at least not since it careened away from public intelligibility. Yet the notion of a main stream in the twentieth century has been grounded in our receiving these hidden structures of subjectivity as "purely musical." This attitude has been responsible for the development of our analytical methods, and it has thus shaped our ways of assessing most of the music we encounter, even though many repertories have had little interest in the subjectivity game.

So long as music that responded to our methods was typed as "purely musical," other ways of making music have been seen as trafficking in the "extramusical," and we either have excluded them from serious consideration or attempted to legitimate them by bracketing their extraneous features and submitting them to organic analysis. Accordingly, Schumann did not dwell on the programmatic dimensions of Berlioz's *Symphonie fantastique* but delivered instead a tortured (though ideologically indispensable) formal account; Allan Forte tried to annex to the Germanic quest for unified subjectivity the aggressively eclectic *Rite of Spring;* and analysts produce Schenkerian graphs of tunes by Jimi Hendrix.[34] But as we pull away from the "purely musical" explanations that favored a particular cluster of composers, when we see their solutions too as conventionally, culturally circumscribed, it becomes easier to find ways of dealing with artists who sought to explore in their music something other than models of unified, autonomous subjectivity. If our methods have been obsessed with discerning hidden depth, the implosion of that model leaves the field open for the increased valuing of alternatives, past and present.

Moreover, I would argue that even the accomplishments of the high serialists become more impressive when their formal devices are understood as part of a representational apparatus that also includes lyrics, references, and the metaphors that grounded those formal devices culturally, that caused the devices to make sense for particular moments in history. I can think of no better model than Richard Taruskin's brilliant discussion of Stravinsky's works, in which forms are interpreted as content, in which cultural agendas and the most abstruse of techniques are demonstrated to be inextricably intertwined.[35]

To remain with "purely musical" accounts even of "absolute" music minimizes our appreciation of why and how these pieces have exerted so much influence, how they negotiated the tensions of their times, why they still matter. And it continues to overlook the ways those underlying structures we often receive as bedrock do cultural work, even when they purport to speak to us from the refuge of counterconvention.

# CHAPTER 5

# Reveling in the Rubble: The Postmodern Condition

To judge from the jeremiads that have circulated in recent years concerning our own moment, we find ourselves now in the aftermath of cultural history—a period often referred to (for better or worse) as Postmodernism. Even those who do not use this word arrive at similar diagnoses: music theorist Robert Morgan, for instance, mourns the disappearance of Donald Tovey's mythological main stream, and Leonard Meyer calls ours a culture of stasis where belief in linear progress has vanished.[1] In one of his most pessimistic essays following World War II, Adorno declared that "to write poetry after Auschwitz is barbaric,"[2] and many historians interpret the poverty of postwar culture as confirming his fatalistic prediction. It would seem that we are condemned to reside in the detritus of history, where nothing of any importance will ever again happen within the cultural arena—at least not in the foreseeable future.

Detractors of Postmodernism like to decry what they regard as the parasitic nature of recent culture. For much of today's art involves the flaunting of signs and conventions lifted from earlier styles—a characteristic especially noteworthy after the fastidious avoidance of public codes under some of the dominant strains of Modernism. Fredric Jameson refers to the dizzying mixtures of recycled codes in the art of our time as pastiche or blank parody ("parody that has lost its sense of humor"),[3] while Jean Baudrillard labels the products of our age "simulacra"—copies that lack originals.[4] Given the fact that conventions have long since been understood as petrified elements no longer capable of participating in expressing anything new, many critics have taken their return as prima facie evidence of surrender, the refusal of contemporary artists to keep up the good fight against cooptation.

This is especially the case with the resurgence in music of the most important convention of them all—namely, tonality. The linear narrative of music history reproduced in textbooks and much critical writing traces the gradual erosion of tonal harmonic syntax over the course of the 1800s and its overthrow by Arnold Schoenberg in the early years of this century. Just as Modernist painters banished representation in favor of abstraction, so avant-garde composers of the early twentieth century came to treat semiotic codes and the principles of harmonic tonality as anathema. Over the course of the last hundred years, a tremendous amount of intellectual energy has been expended on preventing inadvertent lapses back into tonality; although they may seem diametrically opposed philosophically, both serial and chance operations served as precautionary measures, designed to ensure that the deeply ingrained habits of tonal thinking would not creep back into circulation.

Yet despite these Modernist attempts at weeding out all traces of its Other, the paradox remains that atonal projects themselves derive their meaning from tonality. Throughout the years of its exile, tonality was kept simultaneously at bay and in its place of privilege by what Jean-François Lyotard describes as a negative theology: it reigned as the seductive idol against which composers and listeners were expected to practice apostasy.[5] To be sure, some twentieth-century composers (commonly dismissed as reactionaries who failed to participate in the ongoing progressive history of musical innovation) never disavowed tonality or its codes. But it could be argued that those who continued casually to employ its procedures were invested less intensely in tonality than those who based their work on circumventing it at all costs.

The proliferation of triadic sonorities in recent music has thus been received by those faithful to the premises of atonality as backsliding, as if culture had departed suddenly from the rules of a strict diet to engage in a Häagen-Dazs binge; latter-day Modernists voice their righteous indignation in tones that resemble those of ladies from the Temperance Union witnessing the end of Prohibition. Certainly the lushly orchestrated harmonies of, say, David Del Tredici's Alice pieces offer an element of illicit pleasures indulged in with abandon.[6] His Edwardian themes transport us back nostalgically, hedonistically to that time before the ban on tonality: he sutures late Romantic past and Postmodern present seamlessly together, as though the intervening years of Modernist austerity had simply been snipped out. As it says in the Bible, the dog returns to its vomit and the sow that was washed to its wallowing in the mire. And the narrative trajectory of linear progress in the direction of ever-greater abstraction collapses.

But if from the vantage point of high Modernism all instances of Postmodern referentiality sound alike—all equally guilty of betraying the Cause—I want to argue that the practices that have emerged over the last two decades are as vital and varied as those of any other moment in cultural history. For younger generations, today's culture does not lack meaning, nor does it announce the end of history. If our artists no longer heed injunctions against references to cultural codes past and present, this need not signal a passive return to the safety of time-honored clichés. Since the watershed years of the 1960s, many composers have come to believe that music should be "com-posed"—literally, put together—from elements recognizable to a substantial community of listeners, that it should participate in a public arena where interpretation is actively provoked. Yet if that attitude serves as an underlying assumption that informs many musical practices, their commonality ends there. In this chapter, I will take a cluster of very different pieces, all from the last twenty years, all from North America, and discuss briefly how they operate in terms of the codes and conventions with which they engage.

The first segment of Philip Glass's *Glassworks* (1982), "Opening," evokes an earlier era, even more than most pieces by Glass.[7] Not only does it employ triads consistently throughout, but it makes use of the piano, with all its attendant nineteenth-century cultural baggage. Its two-against-three rhythmic figuration, with its implicit melodic lines that appear only hazily from the web of cross-accented triplet patterns, recalls the Romantic piano music of Schumann or Brahms. Moreover, it parses itself out in tidy, symmetrical four-bar periodic phrases.

But no doubt the most retrospective element of this piece is its simulation of an old-fashioned version of subjective interiority. The first phrase sets forth a clear F-minor tonality, and its components suggest an introspective melancholy: its highest voice reaches up tremulously to the fifth degree, its bass line traces most of a descending tetrachord—the age-old emblem of the lament—before a straining major seventh between the top and bottom pitches (C versus D♭) pulls it back to its stoic starting position. By contrast, the second phrase gravitates toward a major-key area (implied E♭) in a lower register, and its falling melodic pattern seems to reach inward, as though to derive its consolation from some source of inner strength; this is a path well trodden by Romantic composers—especially by Schubert, who made these poignant mirages of impossible hope his affective home base. The third phrase contributes conventional signs of yearning (the right-hand A♭ in its second measure produces the expectation of impending arrival on E♭ major) and then disillusion (the pattern sinks back without having found or established what it sought [Ex. 5.1]).

From the point of view of reference, this piece would not work if it failed to push our nineteenth-century semiotic buttons, which still remain (the reformative strategies of Modernism notwithstanding) embarrassingly intact. Before us glimmers once again the Romantic Soul,

Example 5.1: Glass, *Glassworks*, "Opening." Used by permission of Dunvagen Music Publishers.

decked out with all its requisite emotional trappings: alienation, memories of lost arcadia, and longing for utopia. Yet Glass's construction of retro-subjectivity announces itself as a construction, for no sooner does a sentimental gesture tug our sleeve than it becomes somehow decentered. Most often this decentering results from the constant, mechanical repetitions that govern the unfolding of the composition.

For if one was seduced by that vulnerable yearning passage and its poignant deflation the first time around, one surely doesn't fall for it on the third or fourth appearance. If one is tempted by the presentation of a phrase to clasp one's hands to one's bosom in a reflex of Brahmsian autumnal nostalgia, subsequent cycles begin to provoke other reactions. One can, of course (as many do), get irritated at the tease-and-withdraw tactic Glass wields here or at the boredom of too few chords repeated too many times; recall that each strain occurs twelve times in the course of a complete performance. But one can also learn to observe how manipulated one is by musical patterns of this sort; one can begin, in other words, to take apart into components—to deconstruct—these rhetorical devices that still persuade us of their unmediated authenticity in classical concerts or movies.[8]

Alternatively, one may choose to concentrate on the way Glass organizes the experience of time: a way that differs markedly from the goal-oriented trajectories within which we usually find these tonal gestures. *Glassworks'* "Opening" makes us aware of the psychological sequence we expect when we hear triads lined up in this manner, even though none of the strong tonal implications presented in the three strains manages to reach its implied destination; instead, they end equivocally and either circle back to starting position or move on unrequited to the next strain. More important, Glass embeds these harmonic impulses within a Zen-influenced acceptance of cyclic time—the indirect result of the composer's encounters with Asian musics and philosophies. As in some of John Cage's experiments, Glass gives us time frames filled in with repetitious materials; but while Cage arranged his nonstandard materials in accordance with chance operations, Glass selects patterns most dear to our cultural mythology of autonomous subjectivity and rearranges them quite purposefully. Nothing here is left to Chance.

If Glass recalls the music of the centered self and its attendant pleasures, he also sets it adrift. Far from reinhabiting tonality as though we never left it, he recontextualizes it and invites us to notice how its signs work to produce their still-powerful effects. In some sense, what he does may be even more disconcerting to the ability to "believe" in tonality than the actual banishing of it under serialism. For with serialism one was assured that a subject still lurked somewhere in that tormented texture, even if it couldn't be detected: here the self *is* the surface, is nothing *but* surface. Or, depending on how you hear it, Glass takes gestures that used to signify self-absorption and relocates them within a selfless, Zen-oriented time frame. But whatever one's interpretation, this is not tonal business as usual. The signs Glass employs are relatively easy to identify; but what they mean in this particular assemblage is wide open for debate—which is perhaps why he has attracted more impassioned and more sustained controversy than any other of the Minimalists.[9]

If Glass's "Opening" takes a reasonably consistent surface and frustrates our formal expectations, other composers pursue the opposite principle: to present a highly ruptured, eclectic surface that nonetheless traces a perceptible background trajectory. Just as prohibitions against tonality have been overturned recently, so structures based loosely on narrative premises also have made a reappearance. As Teresa de Lauretis has explained, although the program of deconstructing narrative is at times a crucial enterprise, narrative is too important a mode of cultural activity to abdicate altogether. Consequently, we are now witnessing what she refers to as the return of "narrative with a vengeance"—that is, procedures that resemble those that circulated before the Modernist crisis in representation but that now strive, in many cases, to construct new cultural possibilities.[10]

Sometimes the likelihood of finding a coherent narrative in Postmodernist artifacts seems rather remote, as, for instance, in John Zorn's *Spillane* (1986).[11] In the course of the first five minutes of *Spillane*, we hear a woman's scream, a jittery high-hat cymbal introducing a jazz combo, police sirens and dogs barking, another variety of jazz, a gong, a blur of synthesizers and vibes, a strip show complete with noisy patrons—and so it goes for twenty-five minutes.

Music theorist Kofi Agawu titled his study of eighteenth-century classicism (i.e., Haydn and Mozart) *Playing with Signs*,[12] and although I have trouble hearing the pinnacle of classical music as a mere game of signifiers, Zorn's music responds perfectly to that description. It appears to enact the hyperstimulation Baudrillard associates with the *mentalité* of habitual television viewers: the composition resembles a screen upon which images flash by in delirious succession.[13] As Zorn testifies:

I've got an incredibly short attention span. In some sense, it is true that my music is ideal for people who are impatient, because it is jam-packed with information that is changing very fast. But it also takes a little patience because if you get to something you don't like, you have to wait ten seconds or so until it turns into something else. . . . [Y]ou've got to realize that speed is taking over the world. Look at the kids growing up with computers and video games—which are ten times faster than the pinball machines we used to play. There's an essential something that young musicians have, something you can lose touch with as you get older. I love bands like Hüsker Dü, Metallica, Black Flag, Die Kreuzen. Speed bands, thrash bands . . . it's a whole new way of thinking, of living. And we've got to keep up with it. I'll probably die trying.[14]

The disintegrated subject so decried by Modernist theorists of Postmodernism (e.g., Baudrillard and Jameson) here flaunts itself without apology. This is hellzapoppin' nihilism at its best, reveling in the rubble of Western civilization without regrets.

Yet even Zorn, I think, resists falling in line with this cultural diagnosis. The title *Spillane* refers explicitly to the hard-boiled detective novels and *films noirs* of 1940s Los Angeles. To a listener armed with that clue, the sequence of events in the piece makes sense—at least a kind of sense well established within late twentieth-century culture. For if we lack here the tight, organic saga of heroic self-actualization that dominated so much nineteenth-century music, we have nonetheless a narrative schema easily followed by anyone acquainted with urban pulp fiction and the Hollywood movies that translated that genre to the screen.

A woman's scream initiates the action, implying that an act of violence has transpired. Over the course of the piece we trace the progress of the detective not directly through his own feelings (as we would in a typical piece of German Romantic instrumental music) but rather by means of his meanderings through the streets and nightspots of varying degrees of respectability. It is as though we are listening to the soundtrack of a film that doesn't—but easily could—exist. And our anticipation of narrative continuity, formal unity, and closure is gratified when, three-quarters of the way through the piece, another outbreak of screams occurs—this time seven of them, surrounded by the transcendental strains of organ and synth choir, punctuated by machine-gun fire. After this climax, the *dénouement* involves a not-quite-audible conversation in a piano bar, more cool jazz, and an extended, melancholy passage on electric guitar mixed with the sounds of a receding rainstorm.[15] Only here—as is typical of the hard-boiled genre—do we get a glimpse of something like the protagonist's interiority, the existential alienation that marks him as a descendant of the Romantic loner. Thus in spite of all the dislocations of his surface, Zorn returns us to a very familiar version of subjectivity.

Like Hector Berlioz, who tended to present stories obliquely by means of the musical genres encountered by his characters during their odysseys,[16] Zorn's cinematic imagination weaves his structures from musical types with strong public associations. In the case of *Spillane*, he draws on jazz of various sorts, blues, and country, all of which he (a saxophonist of exceptional prowess) and his ensemble of collaborators simulate with uncanny precision.

Their collective virtuosity is far more evident in live concert, for the juxtapositions that sound on recordings like mere splicings are actually performed. On a signal from Zorn, the musicians switch from improvising in the style of one genre to that of another; they hit the ground running without even the slightest hesitation for readjustment.

Yet Zorn emerged from a standard compositional background; he was trained to think in terms of set theory, and he claims as his principal formal influences Stravinsky, Schoenberg, Ives, Partch, Varèse, and Cage.[17] But the manifest content and cinematic qualities of his music acknowledge his debt to African American and pop culture. As he says:

> I grew up in New York City as a media freak, watching movies and
> TV and buying hundreds of records. There's a lot of jazz in me, but

there's also a lot of rock, a lot of classical, a lot of ethnic music, a lot of blues, a lot of movie soundtracks. I'm a mixture of all those things. . . . But jazz is not the tradition in which I feel I can make a significant statement, even though the jazz feeling is essential to me. I believe that improvisation needs to be combined more with composition in order to try creating something new. We should take advantage of all the great music and musicians in this world without fear of musical barriers, which sometimes are even stronger than racial or religious ones. That's the strength of pop music today. It's universal.[18]

Zorn's music announces his refusal to abide by what Andreas Huyssen has called the Great Divide between so-called high and popular culture, for he is heir to both.[19]

To be sure, Zorn adopts here pop genres of the most formulaic variety; elsewhere he grabs onto the genres of Road Runner cartoons and spaghetti Westerns.[20] But it is precisely this relationship with brands of logic already familiar that permits him to experiment with musical form while remaining intelligible. Indeed, as Zorn himself argues in the quotation above, the short attention span, the dizzying collage of myriad jazz and pop styles, and the episodic cycling that characterizes *Spillane* probably qualify as the structures of feeling most typical of our moment, like it or not.

Much of Zorn's music relies on signs of violence for narrative coherence. In *Spillane*, a woman's scream starts the piece and recurs to keep us on track; in "Road Runner," explosions punctuate the episodes, signaling the periodic (though apparently inconsequential) annihilations of the Coyote; in a piece based on the Marquis de Sade, the shrieks of a tortured male victim (performed by the lead singer of Faith No More) organize the action. Expressions of pain become expected structural markers, as they do in our action films, television, and video games; they engage our interest and provide the incentive for our continued attention. The world he presents is no longer the world of eighteenth-century social reconciliation or of nineteenth-century trajectories in which violence erupts only at extreme moments of structural and/or narrative crisis: in Zorn's pieces, so closely related to the dominant media of our moment, violence occurs frequently, even ritually. Far from counting as random assemblages or blank parodies (what we might call "rubble without a cause"), such pieces verge on having an overabundance of meaning, no less so for sounding—sometimes literally—a bit cartoonish.

Yet despite the fact that Zorn's materials—those of both surface and formal background—engage with familiar sounds and genres, the relative accessibility of his pieces does not ensure that he owns their meanings or that they cannot provoke radically different reactions. In 1993, music theorist Ellie Hisama published an article in the journal *Popular Music* in which she analyzed erotic fantasies of Asian women in songs and videos by popular musicians such as David Bowie and John Cougar Mellencamp.[21] The most disturbing part of her article, however, focused on the evocations of Asian women in several of Zorn's pieces, many of which also deploy the violent strategies already noted. Around the time Hisama's article appeared, Zorn pushed his penchant for such fantasies yet further with one album cover (*Torture Garden*) featuring Asian women undergoing sexual torture and another (*Naked City*) depicting a historic form of Chinese capital punishment that involved live dismemberment. Hisama's article had alerted Asian Americans to such imagery, and several representatives from that community began writing critical articles and mounting protests at Zorn's performances.[22]

Zorn does not deny the violence of his visual and musical imagery, which he understands as interconnected; he explains that his graphic images

> have been used for their transgressive quality, illustrative of those areas of human experience hidden in the gaps between pain and pleasure, life and death, horror and ecstasy. . . . When I lived in Japan, I got involved in the S&M torture scene. I lived those images. If someone criticizes me, they're not looking at the scope of my

work, as an artist who deals with these themes in a consistent way. I've used Caucasians in violent situations too.[23]

When pressed for responses to the imagery in *Torture Garden* and *Naked City*, Zorn first insisted on his freedom of expression—his right to explore any kind of subject matter that stimulated his imagination. He finally agreed to have the albums repackaged, and he extended a qualified apology: "As an artist you can't please everyone. If I took all their criticism to heart I'd never create anything. I don't want to make it harder for Asians in this country; I'm on their side. But frankly, I don't think my records are doing that."[24] Many of his colleagues agree and have joined him to protest what they regard as an infringement of Zorn's artistic freedom; Michael Dorf, director of the Knitting Factory (an experimental performance space in New York), claims: "John has artistic integrity. He's got a huge collection of art that has do with this theme. He's done research on it. He's immersed and obsessed with Asian culture. He's not doing this without a consciousness about what it means for women and Asian women and the history of the Japanese exploiting other Asian countries."[25]

This controversy raises several important points. First, no sooner have explicit signifiers returned to art music than they have become subject to public debate and critique. Note that debate in the press is not censorship: the government has not forbidden Zorn from writing and performing his music, even if he has incurred the wrath of a segment of the population that publicly protests his imagery. If art music has been spared such scrutiny for several decades, it is in large part because so little was at stake for either composer or audience. With the return of public codes, however, comes an invitation for public response, as has occurred in Zorn's case.

Second, the rather limited social criticism aimed at Zorn's images of dismemberment pales beside the constant editorials and even congressional hearings on rap music. Yet rap artists, even at their worst, rarely approach Zorn's level of transgression. I would never advocate congressional hearings on Zorn, but I am struck by the differences in broad public reception. Is this difference a result of rap's far greater cultural influence and the relative obscurity of experimentalists—even those few as successful as Zorn? Is art music still insulated from critique by the Romantic ideal of institutionally sanctioned transgression? Has it been, in part, the commercial and cultural irrelevance of most Modernist art music that has exempted it from public scrutiny, merely because it was beneath notice? And does Zorn's bid for communicability remove him from the refuge into which "serious" artists had long ago withdrawn?

Finally, I find it significant that many of the conventions Zorn has reengaged along with several other recent composers—are those associated with narrative violence.[26] Here the distinction between Zorn's and Glass's versions of Postmodernism becomes quite clear: if both utilize triads, they put them together toward very different ends—the former narrative, the latter anti-narrative—with very different cultural implications. Teresa de Lauretis has observed that "narrative demands sadism," and Zorn's return to conventional formal trajectories almost seems calculated to illustrate her point.[27]

Asian American critics mostly indict Zorn's visual images, but their concerns raise implicitly the question of how to deal with musical content in a cultural context that has focused exclusively on style, form, and innovation. Those accounts of Postmodernism that mention collage, eclecticism, and reference without dealing with cultural meanings may shield artistic agendas from debate, but they trivialize their effects. I for one would prefer the widespread controversies that break out over Hollywood movies than the silence that has greeted the premieres of most new music since *Rite of Spring*.

And it is the return to convention—the willingness to operate within codes recognizable to a sizable audience—that makes this music once again worthy of public attention and public disagreement. Perhaps the controversy over Zorn is a sign of success, painful though it may be, rather like a foot that has been asleep and that tingles agonizingly with renewed circulation. As art music manages to attract public attention, it will have to participate in the jostling and friction that always attends the marketplace of competing ideals.

The foregrounding of signifying practices manifested in composers such as Glass and Zorn and the crisis over representation that has erupted in recent cultural studies have occurred at the same time—and far more spectacularly—in popular music. And some aspects of the debates over these practices in popular music bear an uncanny resemblance to those that have taken place in High-Art circles. For in some sense, 1960s rock has come to count in critical circles as the Modernist phase in popular music, fueled as it was with ideas such as progress, authenticity, and rebellion. It was also largely a product of white, male, middle-class youths and entrepreneurs who took the blues and fused it with the familiar nineteenth-century ideals of individualism.

But the emergence of disco in the early 1970s diverted attention away from this aesthetic and toward other kinds of issues. Contrary to the standard account, it isn't so much that pop music became apolitical when the terrain shifted to dance music as that a different cast of characters with very different priorities came to the fore. The mind/body split and the white, male hegemony that had sustained the rock tradition suddenly were called into question by the emergence of groups that had been marginalized, whether because of gender, sexual orientation, or ethnicity. While their expressions gave rise to new formal practices, it took a while for many people to recognize that this was the case, so horrendous was their crime of drawing fans away from rock—especially since their work frequently privileged the body and confounded gender identities. If critics in High-Art circles lamented the betrayal of the Modernist hard line when certain composers reverted to tonality, those invested in popular music became well nigh hysterical when a large segment of the public moved away from rebel rock and embraced the music of black and gay dance clubs. One need only recall the infamous "Disco sucks" campaign, in which listeners were goaded by a

Chicago radio DJ to bring disco records to a local sports arena for a mass burning.[28]

In order to speak from subject positions other than those privileged in rock, however, these new artists had to clear spaces within old conventions, by means of rereadings, fusions, or deconstructions. For the dominant modes of representation available in pop music at the time had been tailored for purposes of rock, and those musical forms were implicated in a project designed to naturalize a particular kind of white, heterosexual masculinity—and thus the focus on signifying practices within recent pop music. Unlike 1960s rockers, who sought to produce the experience of an authentic and autonomous subjectivity (see chapter 2), many of today's artists are both self-conscious and unapologetic about the constructedness of their music and images. Yet such flaunted artificiality does not necessarily imply cynicism; quite the contrary, it can register confidence in the power of human signs to shape social reality. And it has the effect of unmasking anything that tries to present itself as natural, centered, or authentic.

The pop-music artist who has enacted perhaps most obviously the kinds of strategies referred to as Postmodern is the guru of the Minneapolis Sound, the Artist Formerly Known as Prince (henceforth, the Artist). Like J. S. Bach, the Artist developed his style far from the main centers of cultural production; both acquired much of the music that influenced them through commercial distribution networks—Bach through printed scores, the Artist through recordings and radio; and both grafted everything that came their way (whether rococo mannerisms or gangsta rap) onto an increasingly comprehensive and eclectic modus operandi. The Artist picks up from the Beatles, heavy metal, or Nelson Riddle as their devices suit his needs, but his music also constantly refers to, draws on, and reinscribes a rich history of African American music.

In his song "Kiss," for instance, the Artist takes on the blues, with its baggage of unassailable masculinity that inspired British rockers to adopt this African American genre in the 1960s.[29] But it is precisely rock's image of the masculine that he seeks to dislocate in the course of the song. The most obvious risk he takes is to sing in a weirdly vulnerable falsetto, similar to the one honed by Claude Jeter (see chapter 1). This is not the effortless head voice the Artist uses so effectively elsewhere but a sound that is deliberately pinched, as though it is being dammed up for more intense pleasure than that afforded by simple release. It continually threatens to crack downward into normal adult male range, and it is only through the utmost strain, apparently, that he manages to extend this erotic high.

"Kiss" also features a peculiar type of suspended animation the Artist produces when he wants to create the sensation of erotic trance. If the harmonic progression turns out to be that of the standard blues, it may take a while for the listener to detect this, so slow is its unfolding: after the four-bar introductory vamp, it takes the Artist eight additional measures to arrive at the first chord change (the IV that signals that this is indeed a blues, though moving at half-speed) on the third line of the verse. Up until that point, the backdrop had remained resolutely static, as the Artist sings over the same austere instrumental groove that introduced the song. Yet despite the glacial rate of harmonic motion, the rhythmic activity of the song is never still, even though most of it operates on a far more local level than that of the harmonic changes. The surface is constantly agitated by a scratchy groove and a teasing guitar lick that holds itself ambiguous with respect to harmonic context.

"Kiss" sets up a world in which unpredictable titillations, moans, and caresses occupy the foreground, while the chords that guarantee coherence hover as an almost (but not quite) expendable backdrop. Only with the arrival of the chorus ("Don't have to be rich . . . "), which presents the third strain of the blues pattern, do the chords move rapidly enough to attract attention in their own right. Yet the Artist elects not to cycle through V and IV directly to tonic, as the standard blues convention would usually dictate. Instead of yielding immediately to tonic arrival, he proceeds from V and IV to $V^7$ . . . then back again to IV. By presenting the V-to-IV progression twice, he calls greater attention to it as a formula. He thereby undermines conventional certainty that V and IV must in fact lead automatically to I, which intensifies the desire for that resolution.

After a bar on IV and at the moment of greatest tension—the point where the blues progression should finally reach its point of harmonic closure (the final measure of the 12 X 2 it has taken us to get here)—the guitar lick prevents it from taking hold. On the very last beat before the next cycle should restart, the guitar abruptly ceases. And into this naked silence, the Artist drops the word "kiss" with a coy slur that touches on the key note just a split second before the inevitable downbeat. The effect of all these strategies is not delayed gratification: it is a form of quietistic ecstasy that may be sustained indefinitely, but only with tremendous concentration and refusal of thrust or climax or even definitive closure.

As if to make precisely this point, the Artist feigns "losing it" in the final refrain. On the words "Ain't no particular sign," he pushes his already-pinched falsetto up into a kind of white-noise screech, leading to a dramatic deflation. It is as if the discipline involved in maintaining that stoic high finally proves too difficult, and the pent-up energy explodes without his willing it. Yet the suspension of animation is what constitutes the erotic in this song—not the release. At the last moment, the Artist utters "kiss" in a normal speaking voice—stripped, that is, of the tense artifice that has characterized this song—followed by a couple of measures of instrumental fade-out. He thus produces a gap between the persona who sings, who appears to have been overwhelmed at the end of the refrain, and the puppeteer who teasingly stands behind the enactment.

Even the instrumentals participate in this play of indeterminate gender identities. Thus the jangling guitar lick—which precedes the introductory vamp, interrupts the would-be cadence at the end of each chorus, plays the first part of the instrumental chorus, and provides the fade-out at the end—matches the sound and affect of the Artist's pinched falsetto. By contrast, a lewd-sounding wah-wah guitar resembling the Artist's "normal" vocal range takes up the second part of the instrumental chorus, its insinuations saying much more than the lyrics themselves (rather reminiscent of Charlie Green's responses to Bessie Smith's provocations in "Thinking Blues").

The video for "Kiss" makes explicit the gender-bending quality of the song. Although the Artist actually plays all the instruments on the recording, he presents himself in the video in the mode of an exotic singer/dancer fronting a band.[30] He displays his body with a bare midriff and a physical vocabulary typically identified with seductive female entertainers, casts a woman guitar player (long-time bandmember Wendy Melvoin) in the "purely musical" role usually reserved for male musicians, has a woman mouth the occasional low notes, and performs the cryptic hand gestures he has developed to represent female pleasure (the Artist may be the only male musician since the seventeenth century who regularly expresses vaginal envy).[31] Although signs of many kinds of sexual activities occur here in pantomime, they are all highly stylized, almost combinatorial in effect—anything but natural—yet bizarrely erotic.

If the Artist unsettles standard representations of masculinity in "Kiss," he does not do so in all his music. His menagerie of sexual types also contains constructions such as "Gett Off," with its pile-driving downbeats, or the leering, heavy-metal spray-downs of "Electric Chair"; but it also includes slow-hand seductions such as "Insatiable" and the giddy, polymorphous perversity of "Cream."[32] Each of these presents a different groove, a different sensibility, a different way of experiencing the body, pleasure, gender. If masculinity no longer stands as a stable entity after one has heard his music,[33] the Artist offers in its place the experience of gender and sexuality as performance—always mutable, always open to invention.[34] If this is Postmodern decentered subjectivity, then it ain't half bad.

Canadian musician k.d. lang is another prominent perpetrator of what Arthur Kroker has called "sign crimes" in the gender/sexuality department.[35] As the title of her album *Absolute Torch and Twang* indicates, lang occupies a peculiar position between country music and romantic ballads, and her 1992 album, *Ingenue*, continues her exploration and fusions of unlikely pop genres.[36] Throughout her career, many of lang's fans have perceived her as speaking from a lesbian subject-position, in part because of her intricate manipulations of received musical types and their associated gender ideologies. Strikingly, hers is not the folk-based, "naturalized" discourse of women's music produced in the early phases of the feminist movement, which treated gender and sexuality as though they were unproblematic givens for purposes of consolidating a unified community. Instead, lang belongs to a younger generation that believes that one cannot speak directly from a lesbian or even a woman's vantage point, that one can only inhabit, destabilize, and somehow try to make a new kind of sense by means of previously existing codes.

In her song "Still Thrives This Love," for instance, lang adopts the trappings of a Latin ballad—a convention that quickly signals steamy romantic encounters but is heavily laden with camp connotations. Too many cartoon characters and drag queens have clamped roses between their teeth, flounced their ruffled skirts, and danced a couple of steps of the tango for anyone to take this discourse seriously. Moreover, as the song continues, it picks up the hackneyed sounds of a sultry Parisian accordion and tilts toward the Neapolitan sentimentality of "O sole mio." And yet, how does one speak of love in a Postmodern universe—especially when not only love but also gender and sexuality are profoundly unstable?

K.D. LANG, "STILL THRIVES THIS LOVE," *Ingenue* (1992)

I often wonder
Is it so
All I am holding
Wants to let go
How could I manage
I don't know

I often question
Is it so
Life's contradictions
Tend to grow
Spawning the choices
And the woe

But, still somehow thrives this love
Which I pray I'm worthy of
Still somehow thrives this love

I often wonder
Is it so
The lessons of patience
Are learned slow
And earnings of labour
May never show

But, still somehow, [etc.]

*k.d. lang, "Still Thrives This Love." Words and music by k.d. lang and Ben Mink. © Copyright 1992 by Polygram International Publishing, Inc., and Zavion Entertainment, Inc. (ASCAP). International copyright secured. Used by permission. All rights reserved.*

Well, lang embraces it with gusto, complete with all its silliness and theatricality, and tries somehow to make it work nonetheless. Like the artful, ambiguous performances of Billie Holiday, lang's inflections twist incessantly: sometimes she undermines the musical impulse by delivering the wrong modal mediant, sometimes she rings out lines as though from the depth of her heart. She doesn't entirely trust the language she has chosen, but she also knows that she cannot speak from outside language; and rather than opting for noncommunication, she sings on defiantly, demonstrating most poignantly the pathos, the absurdity, the hilarity of uttering something as shop-worn as an admission of love: love, which still somehow lingers on long after cynical intellectuals have announced the demise of centered subjectivity.

lang's declaration of love is tinged with embarrassment, as it admits the possibility of still experiencing such remnants of an outdated ideology; the script she takes up is thoroughly compromised by its history in heterosexual romantic kitsch. Yet she broadcasts it nonetheless, singing on the borderline between irony and sincerity, between ambivalence and hope. As she breaks open those obsolete bottles for containing obsolete, woefully clichéd feelings, she manages somehow to infuse them with new wine.

The musical genre that epitomizes the process of fusion I have been describing—that has taken it far beyond anything that could be considered a random play of signifiers and into political terrains so sensitive that it has provoked censorship—is rap, the musical component of hip-hop culture. Originating in the urban blight of the South Bronx in the 1970s, rap quickly spread to the black neighborhoods of Los Angeles and Oakland; by the 1990s, communities of rap artists had emerged all over the globe. It constitutes perhaps the most vital area of popular music today.

As cultural theorist Tricia Rose has argued, the music of hip-hop is grounded both in the history of African American culture and in the latest technological developments.[37] On the one hand, the lyrics and their modes of performance trace their lineage back to the *griots* of West Africa, to the virtuosic, competitive language games of the streets such as toasts or the dozens. But on the other hand, rap has always drawn much of its creative energy from the mediating devices of the recording industry. Whether this involves playing two turntables off each other in ways never envisioned by manufacturers, producing percussive effects by rhythmically scratching the surfaces of revolving LPs, sampling recorded materials and reassembling them into collages, or ferreting out and exploiting the noise-enhancing capabilities of samplers and multitrack recorders, rap artists turn machines invented for preserving music into musical instruments. Technology itself is subjected to the practices of signifying.

The romantic search for authenticity is thus frustrated in advance by this music that foregrounds its own fundamental mediation. Yet any attempt at writing it off as the mechanical result of automatic devices runs up against a whole network of African American practices: namely the emphasis on powerful physical rhythms, on call/response, on individual virtuosity enfolded in community. In fact, one of the most important features of rap involves its intense concern with reference—the actual incorporation of moments from the history of recorded black music, made possible through sampling. While this device has sometimes been dismissed as evidence of rap's lack of originality, most samples principally act as pretexts for the intertextual signifying so central to African-based practices. More than that, they reflect an obsession with cultural memory, a desire to transmit traces of the past as still-vibrant elements of the present. Rap offers the black community its own version of music history texts.

So far, who could object? Of course, the controversy surrounding rap arises from the fact that some artists articulate aggressively a whole range of taboo subjects: not only grievances over police brutality, economic injustice, and anti-black racism but also the explicit misogyny, homophobia, and anti-Semitic prejudices nurtured by some black youths. Rap is far from monolithic, however; in fact, it includes far more internal critique than any other genre I know, as the excesses of a particular group are quickly answered by others of the community— not just on paper but in raps that challenge, for instance, debased depictions of women. But although I could cite many instances of affirmative rap, I do not want to explain away the insistent noise and confrontational attitudes frequently voiced in rap: they are the expressions of a diverse community that is often very angry. And to ignore this extraordinary form because it sounds unpleasant is to risk being caught by surprise—as with the events in Los Angeles in 1992—when those frustrations ignite. It is also to overlook some of the most important and most innovative music of our time.

When I first spoke to musicologists about rap in 1990, I was chastised for playing it safe by discussing Queen Latifah—the politically impeccable leader of women rappers.[38] I don't apologize for having chosen Latifah at that time: she was then among the most powerful of rap artists, and besides, I wanted to be able to elicit a somewhat sympathetic response from an audience that associated rap only with the excesses of 2 Live Crew or the anti-Semitic Professor Griff.[39] For purposes of this chapter I will discuss Public Enemy, a group from Long Island that has often been in the center of controversy, in part because their exceptional artistry makes so much more potent whatever it is they express.

Public Enemy's tune "Nighttrain" (*Apocalypse 91: The Enemy Strikes Black*) takes as its point of departure a song of the same name by the musician perhaps most heavily cited in rap, James Brown.[40] Brown often selected his own song "Night Train" for the closing number in his shows: an up-tempo instrumental blues, it left Brown free to pull out the stops on his spectacular dance routines. His voice breaks in only to coax listeners on board, to recite the names of cities that would resonate with the experiences of his black audience, and to croon "carry me home."

If Brown's image of the night train means to pull a dispersed community together, Chuck D's lyrics in the Public Enemy tune fracture that dream by redefining the night train as the social perception that lumps all blacks together—thieves and drug dealers with those trying to fashion a better world. It is a harshly critical song, one that breaks rank with unquestioned solidarity and that advocates that the community distance itself from those who would destroy the common good. Of course, it also reveals bitter hostility for a racist society that judges all African Americans for the crimes of a few, just because "some of them look just like you." But "Nighttrain" also extends a call for self-criticism, and it especially indicts behaviors celebrated by the subgenre of gangsta rap. And in the final section, Chuck D identifies himself with the night train, the black community, in counterdistinction to those who have forgotten their constituencies. It is a complex song that simultaneously resists black essentialism while it embraces the need for political coalition. When Brown's samples emerge, they are saturated with irony, as his celebration of good times finds itself juxtaposed with the dystopic world northern urban migration has in fact produced.

I want to mention one other important reference in "Nighttrain." The tune opens with a dissonant horn blast that can be heard simply as imitating a train. But this blast is sampled from the beginning of Blood, Sweat & Tears' 1960s hit "Spinning Wheel": a song about a merry-go-round that offers a laissez-faire approach to life. After the horn blast in the original, a loopy beat emerges over which a laid-back voice advocates that we "grab a painted pony, let the spinning wheel spin." Compare that with the beginning of "Nighttrain." After the blast, Public Enemy's production crew (the Bomb Squad) lays down an aggressive groove that backs off, then plows decisively into each successive downbeat. James Brown's voice is heard deep in the mix, his "night train" used as overlapping impulses to create cross-accents. Over this, Flavor Flav hectors Brown to give up his seat, finally handing the reins over to Chuck D. We don't need to recognize the references to make sense of "Nighttrain," but knowing them adds several layers of irony. If the sample leads you to anticipate the druggy lope of "Spinning Wheel," for instance, Public Enemy's groove broadsides you—catches you right upside the head.

More than most rappers, Chuck D brings to his lyrics the consummate rhythmic sensibility of a gospel preacher or a bebop virtuoso.[41] Far from delivering regimented lines with end-rhymes predictably confirming the meter, his poetry is designed from the outset to maximize its rhythmic impact in performance. Its obliqueness results not only from its consistent use of expressions and references that circulate mostly within the urban ghetto but also from his penchant for sacrificing straightforward prose for the sake of spiraling puns and rapid-fire clusters of internal rhymes. Even if doing this sometimes obscures the literal sense of the message, the muscular rhetoric such devices produce more than compensates: in his ability to control pacing, momentum, and accent in underscoring his points he has no peer. And although Chuck D's poetry sometimes becomes as elliptical as that of late Mallarmé, it is important to keep in mind that it is comprehended and even memorized by huge numbers of fans, white as well as black.

In the text below, I have indicated where the downbeats fall in relation to Chuck D's rap. In the section before the first break, he frequently begins right after the downbeat, as though the beat pushes him into action. But as the lyrics proceed, his enjambments increasingly overrun the barlines, and in the final stretch, he dodges the dictates of the meter consistently until he pauses to set up his final line. Note especially the dizzying cross-rhythms produced in lines 62–65, in which his rhymes of talk, walk, New York, then lack, attack, black, crack, and back lay down aggressive accents that threaten to overpower the groove. He then backs off chillingly for the crucial lines "I test a friend wit' sincerity . . . or consider him an enemy." Even the groove halts here, set back in motion only when Chuck D slams into what is in this song an unusual downbeat opening on "Who am I . . . "

The section I label as the refrain brings back James Brown's invitation to get on board, mixed with a sample of a woman saying "stop the train!" and the voice of a porter barking orders. The groove is stripped down to a kind of suspended animation for these sections, always in preparation for Chuck D's next onslaught. A vaguely blues-like bass alternation articulates the junctures between verse and refrain, between refrain and break, between important segments of the rap. And throughout, the production team layers on noise: the noise of trains, noise of the street, noise for the sake of noise. "Nighttrain" isn't meant to be pretty, and the factors we usually trace as musical are deliberately kept to a minimum. But the concentration of physical energy, rhythmic virtuosity, cultural reference, and social critique produced here is stunning.

PUBLIC ENEMY: "NIGHTTRAIN,"
*Apocalypse 91: The Enemy Strikes Black* (1991)

Land of the *free*
But the skin I'm in identifies me
—So the people around me
Energize me
5  *Call*in' all aboard this train ride
Talkin' 'bout *raw* hardcore
Leavin' frauds on the outside
—But the bad thing is anyone can ride the train
—And the reason
10  For that is 'cause we look the same
*Look*in' all around at my so called friend
Light *skin* to the brown
The black
Here we go again
15  *Hom*ey over there knows Keith an
But he be *thief*in'
I don't trust him
Rather bust 'em
*Up* out goes his hand and I cough
20  He once *stole* from me
Yeah I wanna cut it off
—The black thing it's a ride I call the nighttrain
—It rides the good and the bad
We call the monkey trained
25  *Trained* to attack the black it's true
'Cause some of them look just like you
[REFRAIN]
Stayin' *on* the scene
Sittin' on the train
—See all the faces
30  Look about the same
There go the *sell*out who's takin' a ride like Cargo
—'Cause he deal

The keys from Key Largo
—Runnin' Nat narcotic
35 By George he *got* it
Takin' makin' the G erotic
And the *fiends* they scheme
So he can put 'em down
But his *meth*od is wreck 'em
40 Put 'em in tha ground
Got tha *nerve* as hell
To yell brother man
He ain't *black* man
But he ain't his black man
45 Known to *mur*der his own
Traitor on the phone
Ridin' the *train*
Self-hater trained
To sell pain
50 The *mas*ter's toy
His little boy
Hard to *avoid* he look wit' it but he null 'n' void
'Cause he *rid*in' the train you think he down for the cause
—'Cause his face looks just like yours
[REFRAIN; BREAK]
55 More of the *same* insane who sayin'
Like flowin' like *night*train
Runnin' the pain of the black reign
—You look, you laugh
You doubt and go out
60 And I'm *gone*
But the bass goes on
To *talk* the talk, walk the walk
The king of New *York*
Crack a lack attack the black
65 To crack the *back*
Once again I test a friend wit' *sin*cerity

Or consider him an enemy
*Who* am I to tell a lie
Rather push da *bush*
70 Hope da cracker get crushed
I'm rollin' wit' *rush*
Leader of the bum rush
Russian I *ain't*
Spreadin' like paint
75 Lookin' at the *put* I got
And its kickin'
But it ain't *chick*en
But it's livin' for a city
So sick 'n' *tired*
80 Of a scene buckwild, piled in a *file*
Senile or chile
They said it never *been* no worser
Than this, I'm on the night *train*
They hope ya don't miss it
85 Give ya what dey *got*ta give you just go
You musn't just *put* your
Trust in every brother yo
Some don't *give* a damn
'Cause they the other man
90 Worse than a *bomb*
Posin' as Uncle Tom
Dis*grac*in' the race
Blowin' up
The whole crew
95 —Wit' some of them lookin'
Just like you.
[REFRAIN]

*"Nighttrain" by Carlton Ridenhour, Hank Shocklee, Keith Shocklee, and Gary Rinaldo. © 1991 Reach Back (BMI), a division of Reach Music International, Inc.; Suburban Funk, Inc. (BMI) (administered by Reach Back); and Def American Songs, Inc.*

I started this book with an anecdote concerning gurus, and I'll conclude with another—this one from a cartoon by R. Crumb that was displayed in the Harvard Philosophy Department Library in the early 1970s. A weary disciple reaches the mountain peak to find Mr. Natural, the long-bearded character whose admonition "Keep on truckin!" remains an icon of that moment in history. In response to the question, "What does it all mean, Mr. Natural?" the guru declares: "Don't mean shit." In the aftermath of the all-too-meaningful 1960s, Mr. Natural's slogan became an easy way for cynics to dismiss virtually everything. If there could be no poetry after Auschwitz, there could be no meaning of any kind after the decline of the counterculture. And the torch of pessimism passes from Adorno to Mr. Natural to the age-group now known as Generation X. In the doomsday words of Fredric Jameson:

> Hence, once again, pastiche: in a world in which stylistic innovation is no longer possible, all that is left is to imitate dead styles, to speak through the masks and with the voices of the styles in the imaginary museum. But this means that contemporary or postmodernist art is going to be about art itself in a new kind of way; even more it means that one of its essential messages will involve the necessary failure of art and the aesthetic, the failure of the new, the imprisonment in the past.[42]

Elsewhere, however, Jameson himself quotes Nietzsche's reminder concerning the impossibility of thought outside "the prison-house of language";[43] I would extend this principle to suggest that we must likewise cease to produce art if we refuse to do it in the prison-house of the past: that is, with reference to the conventions that still serve as repositories for cultural beliefs and ideals. For it ought to be clear by now that I see a great deal of reveling going on in today's musical culture and that very little of our culture truly resembles rubble, even when its elements proclaim themselves as having been recycled from the rubbish bin of history. Far from being a time of failed art or the imitation of dead styles, it is a moment, I believe, of exuberant creativity, even when (perhaps especially when) its art refers most brazenly to earlier traditions.

As much as they differ one from another, each of the musicians I have discussed in this chapter—from Philip Glass to k.d. lang to Chuck D—is concerned with performing some active negotiation with the cultural past for the sake of here and now. And that cultural past includes only as one of its tributaries the classical-music tradition. If, as we move into the next century, musicologists are to be able to account for the 1900s, we need to be able to grasp present-day musical culture in all its complexity. And that means being prepared to recognize the structures of feeling underlying many different repertories, as well as their processes of dynamic change and their strategic fusions.[44]

I have left out of my discussion (among many other worthy issues) the enormous issue of cross-cultural fusions that are so central a part of today's music scene. Whether they involve the borrowing of non-Western elements in music composed in and for the Western market (the "World Music" bins in record stores) or the responses from all over the globe—from Africa, the Caribbean, India—to American popular music, such hybrids bring with them a set of complex political issues that would require extensive treatment. But these phenomena too constitute an integral part of our collective world now, and they ought to show up in any survey of contemporary "Western" music.[45]

The more one understands music in these terms, the less it is possible to hold onto any notion of absolutes from the past. Admittedly, today's culture does not seem to be coalescing into a linear main stream, nor does it by any means represent the arrival at a utopian vision, but neither is it mired in stasis or in passive nostalgia. Instead of searching vainly for continuous "authentic" traditions, we need to pay attention to the kinds of ferment located in boundaries, to fusions of unpredictable sorts that continually give rise to new genres and modes of expression.

If I tend to reread the European past in my own Postmodern image, if I frequently write about Bach and Beethoven in the same ways in which I discuss the Artist Formerly Known as Prince and John Zorn, it is not to denigrate the canon but rather to show the power of music all through its history as a signifying practice. For this is how culture always works—always grounded in codes and social contracts, always open to fusions, extensions, transformations. To me, music never seems so trivial as in its "purely musical" readings. If there was at one time a rationale for adopting such an intellectual position, that time has long since past. And if the belief in the nineteenth-century notion of aesthetic autonomy continues to be an issue when we study cultural history, it can no longer be privileged as somehow true.

The problem is not so much that a dependable linear main stream has collapsed as that there never was such a thing, except in fictions constructed after the fact—and always for particular ideological purposes. Modernists fear that our present moment represents the end of history. But I would claim that Postmodernism—with its rejection of entrenched master narratives—demands of us a far more diversified way of telling the history of music than we have previously permitted ourselves to entertain: a history that includes medieval liturgists, Renaissance courtiers, Austrian symphonists, Canadian country/western singers, and rappers from Long Island, a history of perpetual bricolage and fusions of hand-me-down codes and conventions—a history in which Western musicians have always been reveling in the rubble.

# NOTES

## PREFACE

1. Susan McClary, *Feminine Endings: Music, Gender, and Sexuality* (Minneapolis: University of Minnesota Press, 1991).

2. Madonna, "Human Nature," *Bedtime Stories* (Maverick, 1994).

3. I am finally getting back to sixteenth and seventeenth century repertories in the context of two books: *First Book of Madrigals: Studies in Renaissance Subjectivity* and *Power and Desire in Seventeenth-Century Music*.

## CHAPTER 1: TURTLES ALL THE WAY DOWN
## (ON THE "PURELY MUSICAL")

1. After I delivered the Bloch Lectures, I found that several other writers had drawn recently on the same story. Stephen Hawking uses it to open *A Brief History of Time: From the Big Bang to Black Holes* (New York: Bantam Books, 1988), 1. He tells a different version, albeit with the same punch line. Clifford Geertz relates the story in *The Interpretation of Culture* (New York: Basic Books, 1973), 28–29, and Judith Becker and Lorna McDaniel also employ it in "A Brief Note on Turtles, Claptrap, and Ethnomusicology," *Ethnomusicology* 35 (1991): 393–98. "Turtles all the way down" thus appears to have become a *locus classicus*—a particularly popular nugget of conventional wisdom—in this age of eroding certainties.

2. See, for example, Susan McClary, *Feminine Endings: Music, Gender, and Sexuality* (Minneapolis: University of Minnesota Press, 1991); "Narratives of Bourgeois Subjectivity in Mozart's 'Prague' Symphony," in *Understanding Narrative*, ed. James Phelan and Peter Rabinowitz (Columbus: Ohio State University Press, 1994), 65–98; "The Impromptu That Trod on a Loaf: Or How Music Tells Stories," *Narrative* 5 (1997): 20–35; and "'Same as It Ever Was': Youth Culture and Music," in *Microphone Fiends: Youth Music and Youth Culture*, ed. Andrew Ross and Tricia Rose (New York: Routledge, 1994), 29–40.

3. Equivalents of the "purely musical" exist also in the other arts. Zola, for instance, justified Manet's scandalous *Olympia* as "pure painting," thus erasing from consideration the disturbing content of that canvas. See the discussion in Charles Bernheimer, "The Uncanny Lure of Manet's *Olympia*," in *Seduction and Theory: Readings of Gender, Representation, and Rhetoric*, ed. Dianne Hunter (Urbana: University of Illinois Press, 1989), 16.

4. For more on this particular convention, see my "Gender Ambiguities and Erotic Excess in Seventeenth-Century Venetian Opera," in *Actualizing Absence: Performance, Visuality, Writing*, ed. Mark Franko and Annette Richards (Hanover, N.H.: Wesleyan University Press, 1999).

5. Conventions have been taken rather more seriously in a couple of areas of recent musicology. When scholars began to study nineteenth-century Italian opera in the 1980s, they had to learn to overcome the (largely German) prejudice against conventions and to focus on the ways Rossini or Verdi operated productively within shared procedures. Similarly, specialists in the eighteenth century have demonstrated the importance of topoi and conventions in the classic repertory. See, for instance, Wye Jamison Allanbrook, *Rhythmic Gesture in Mozart* (Chicago: University of Chicago Press, 1992). See also *Convention in Eighteenth- and Nineteenth-Century Music: Essays in Honor of Leonard G. Ratner*, ed. Wye Jamison Allanbrook, Janet M. Levy, and William P. Mahrt (Stuyvesant, N.Y.: Pendragon Press, 1992). Most of this work concentrates on structures of deliberate signification or particular formal devices rather than on the elements commonly understood as "purely musical."

6. Lydia Goehr's Bloch Lectures present a sympathetic account of the political and philosophical rationales behind the nineteenth-century notion of the "purely musical." See her *The Quest for Voice: Music, Politics, and the Limits of Philosophy* (Berkeley and Los Angeles: University of California Press, 1998).

Despite what may at first glance appear as opposing positions, Goehr and I tend to agree about the history of this concept and also about the ways in which it has reified into a prohibition against cultural interpretation. For an exceptionally thoughtful treatment of the impact of such attitudes on nineteenth-century musical practice, see Leonard B. Meyer, *Style and Music: Theory, History, and Ideology* (Philadelphia: University of Pennsylvania Press, 1989).

7. For an investigation of similar longings to escape cultural contingency and to locate speech in the metaphysical, see Umberto Eco, *The Search for the Perfect Language*, trans. James Fentress (Oxford: Blackwell, 1995).

8. Hayden White, *The Content of the Form: Narrative Discourse and Historical Representation* (Baltimore: Johns Hopkins University Press, 1987). See also his "Form, Reference, and Ideology in Musical Discourse," afterword to *Music and Text: Critical Inquiries*, ed. Steven Paul Scher (Cambridge: Cambridge University Press, 1992).

9. Raymond Williams, *Marxism and Literature* (Oxford: Oxford University Press, 1977), 128–35; Fredric Jameson, *The Political Unconscious: Narrative as a Socially Symbolic Act* (Ithaca: Cornell University Press, 1981); Roland Barthes, *Mythologies*, trans. Annette Lavers (New York: Hill and Wang, 1972); Thomas S. Kuhn, *The Structure of Scientific Revolutions* (Chicago: University of Chicago Press, 1962); Kaja Silverman, "The Dominant Fiction," in her *Male Subjectivity at the Margins* (New York: Routledge, 1992); Ross Chambers, *Story and Situation: Narrative Seduction and the Power of Fiction* (Minneapolis: University of Minnesota Press, 1984), chapter 1.

10. Arnold Schoenberg, *Theory of Harmony* (1911), trans. Roy E. Carter (Berkeley and Los Angeles: University of California Press, 1983), 128–29 and *passim*. Claudio Monteverdi's famous polemic opens his *Fifth Book of Madrigals* (1605); a gloss on this text by his brother, Giulio Cesare, followed in the 1607 publication of *Scherzi musicali*. For a translation of the glossed text, see Oliver Strunk, ed., *Source Readings in Music History* (New York: Norton, 1950), 405–12.

11. Fred Maus has complained that an excessive amount of attention has been expended by the discipline on pieces that utilize moves to the minor submediant. See his "Music as Narrative," *Indiana Theory Review* 12 (1991): 20. As one of those guilty of writing extensively on this phenomenon and other "deviant" devices that seem to demand interpretation, I intend to do penance in this book by addressing the other side of the coin.

12. For the classic critique of this position, see Joseph Kerman, "How We Got into Analysis, and How to Get Out," in *Write All These Down: Essays on Music* (Berkeley and Los Angeles: University of California Press, 1994), 12–32.

13. Plato, *The Republic*, 424c.

14. See my "Music, the Pythagoreans, and the Body," in *Choreographing History*, ed. Susan Leigh Foster (Bloomington: Indiana University Press, 1995), 82–104. See also Eco, *The Search for the Perfect Language*.

15. Theodor W. Adorno, "Music and Language: A Fragment," in *Quasi una Fantasia: Essays on Modern Music*, trans. Rodney Livingstone (London: Verso, 1992), 6. I wish here to acknowledge once again my debt to the work of Adorno and his foremost American explicator, Rose Rosengard Subotnik.

16. For a remarkable study that reconstitutes dominant meanings before it destabilizes them, see Rose Rosengard Subotnik, "How Could Chopin's A-Major Prelude Be Deconstructed?," in *Deconstructive Variations: Music and Reason in Western Society* (Minneapolis: University of Minnesota Press, 1996), 39–147. See also Lawrence Kramer, *Music as Cultural Practice, 1800–1900* (Berkeley and Los Angeles: University of California Press, 1990) and *Classical Music and Postmodern Knowledge* (Berkeley and Los Angeles: University of California Press, 1995).

17. For more on Stradella's flamboyant life, see Carolyn Gianturco, *Alessandro Stradella, 1639–1682* (New York: Oxford University Press, 1994). Stradella composed principally for Roman and northern Italian patrons; *La Susanna* premiered in 1681, the year before Stradella was assassinated in retaliation for the last of his ill-fated seductions.

18. For an analysis of Susanna-and-the-elders conventions, see Mary D. Garrard, "Artemisia and Susanna," in *Feminism and Art History*, ed. Norma Broude and Mary D. Garrard (New York: Harper and Row, 1982), 147–72.

Long before feminist critics launched their critiques, however, Denis Diderot addressed candidly the problem of Susanna representations: "I look at Susannah, and far from feeling abhorrence toward the elders, perhaps I have wished to be in their place" (*Pensées détachées*, 767, as translated in Michael Fried, *Absorption and Theatricality: Painting and the Beholder in the Age of Diderot* [Berkeley and Los Angeles: University of California Press, 1980], 96). Diderot elsewhere absolves his complicity thus: "An Italian painter composed this subject very ingeniously. He placed the two elders on the same side. Susannah covers herself with all her veils on that side, with the result that in order to escape the elders' gaze she exposes herself entirely to the eyes of the beholder. This composition is very free and no one is offended by it. It is because the obvious intention saves everything and because the beholder is never part of the subject. . . . It is the difference between a woman who is seen and a woman who exhibits herself" (*Salons*, II and III, quoted in Fried, *Absorption and Theatricality*, 97).

19. The testo's text reads as follows:

La bella Donna intanto sul' verde pavimento movea le molli piante, Ambiano l'erbe di prostrarsi al sue piè, parea che ì fiori apostati del sole a la novella luce chi nassero idolatri le cervici odorose—

Ad'ammantar le rose parea che dà i bei labri fossero travenate le propore più fine, e saggessero i gigli entro quel seno di più puro candor tepide brine.

Giunta la Donna ove svenato un'sasso in conco d'alabrastro spande lubrico argento, dove frondoso cerro briareo vegetante con cento briaccia e cento l'ingresso al sol contende, e da curiosi rai mantenitor dell'ombra il rio difende—

Ivi tuffa nell'acque il petto ignudo e sirena del Ciel dentro il liquido gel così confonde crome di foco a l'armonia dell' onde.

I used the testo's recitative, the interchange between the elders, Susanna's *scena*, and her lament in prison as the principal components in my music-theater piece *Susanna Does the Elders* (Southern Theater, Minneapolis, 1987). A full recording of the oratorio, directed by Alan Curtis, is available on Reflexe 1C 165–45 643/44.

20. For instance, see my discussion of Monteverdi's "Zefiro torna," in "Music, the Pythagoreans, and the Body."

21. For an examination of procedure in a particular sixteenth-century madrigal, see my discussion of Arcadelt's "Il bianco e dolce cigno" in "Music, the Pythagoreans, and the Body." For an account of the shift between sixteenth- and seventeenth-century procedures, see my *The Transition from Modal to Tonal Organization in the Works of Monteverdi* (Ann Arbor: UMI, 1976).

22. See chapter 3 for a discussion of the kinds of cultural work performed by the da capo aria.

23. Recall, for instance, Bach's Brandenburg Concerto No. 5, in which a seicento-style harpsichord cadenza threatens to overpower the movement's formal order. See my "The Blasphemy of Talking Politics during Bach Year,"

in *Music and Society: The Politics of Composition, Performance, and Reception*, ed. Richard Leppert and Susan McClary (Cambridge: Cambridge University Press, 1987), 13–62.

24. For more on the context within which this music flourished, see José Antonio Maravall, *Culture of the Baroque: Analysis of a Historical Structure*, trans. Terry Cochran (Minneapolis: University of Minnesota Press, 1986); Michel de Certeau, *The Mystic Fable*, vol. 1, *The Sixteenth and Seventeenth Centuries*, trans. Michael B. Smith (Chicago: University of Chicago Press, 1992); Debora Kuller Shuger, *The Renaissance Bible: Scholarship, Sacrifice, and Subjectivity* (Berkeley and Los Angeles: University of California Press, 1994); and Richard Rambuss, *Closet Devotions* (Durham, N.C.: Duke University Press, 1998).

25. *The Life of Saint Teresa of Avila by Herself*, trans. J. M. Cohen (London: Penguin Books, 1957), 210.

26. See again my *Transition in the Works of Monteverdi*.

27. See my "Constructions of Gender in the Dramatic Works of Monteverdi," in *Feminine Endings*, and Wendy Heller, "The Queen as King: Refashioning Semiramide for *Seicento* Venice," *Cambridge Opera Journal*, 5, no. 2 (July 1993): 93–114. Heller is writing a book on seventeenth-century operatic femmes fatales for University of California Press.

28. Recall Bernini's statue of St. Teresa, Richard Crashaw's "Hymn to Sainte Teresa," or the setting of "Anima mea liquefacta est" by Schütz in his *Symphoniae Sacrae I*.

29. For more on this excess-and-frame mechanism in conjunction with representations of femininity, see McClary, *Feminine Endings*, Chapter 4.

30. As Jeter explains, "After we went commercial, every thirteen weeks we got a raise. We stayed five and a half years, and by then we were making pretty good change" (quoted in Anthony Heilbut, *The Gospel Sound: Good News and Bad Times*, 3d ed. [New York: Limelight Editions, 1989], 118).

31. Even when they were living as professionals, their lot was not an easy one. Jeter reports that, "Often we had to send home for money for our hotels. We'd get to programs, the doors be locked, and the promoter split town. You know that part still happens today" (quoted in Heilbut, *Gospel Sound*, 119).

32. Available on *Get Right with the Swan Silvertones* (Rhino RNLP 70081).

33. See Christopher Small, *Music of the Common Tongue: Survival and Celebration in African-American Music* (London, 1987; Hanover, N.H.: Wesleyan University Press, 1998).

34. Christopher Small's latest book argues that ALL musical practices ought to be defined in this way. See *Musicking: The Meanings of Performing and Listening* (Hanover, N.H.: Wesleyan University Press, 1998). Lydia Goehr arrives at something like this definition as well: "If, furthermore, we were to take seriously the idea that music is composed by composers in order to be performed by performers and heard by audiences, we would soon move our interest away from a narrowly formalist concern with works and the question of their formed content and fix it more on the matter of people engaging with music as either an individual or social assertion of their freedom—their subjective freedom . . . to be musical" (*Quest for Voice*, 17).

35. Henry Louis Gates Jr., *The Signifying Monkey: A Theory of African-American Literary Criticism* (Oxford: Oxford University Press, 1988), *passim*.

36. Small makes this point throughout *Music of the Common Tongue*, as does LeRoi Jones (later Amiri Baraka) in his *Blues People: The Negro Experience in White American and the Music That Developed From It* (New York: Morrow Quill, 1963), *passim*.

37. See John S. Mbiti, *African Religions and Philosophy*, 2d ed. (Oxford: Heinemann, 1989). Earlier moments in European practice also privileged ideas such as the alignment through music of body and soul or the simulation in music of transcendental rapture. See, for instance, Gary Tomlinson, *Music in Renaissance Magic* (Chicago: University of Chicago Press, 1993).

38. See Lawrence W. Levine, *Black Culture and Black Consciousness: Afro-American Folk Thought from Slavery to Freedom* (Oxford: Oxford University Press, 1977), 189, for a discussion of the central importance of gospel's rhythmic dimensions.

39. Claude Jeter, in interview with Kerri Rubman, quoted in liner notes by Ray Funk for *Get Right with the Swan Silvertones*.

40. Jeter, quoted in Heilbut, *Gospel Sound*, 116.

41. Jeter, quoted in Heilbut, *Gospel Sound*, 116.

42. Of the weirdness of his falsetto, Jeter says: "I've never imitated a woman in my falsetto. There's a difference. When some people want to laugh, rather than say I sound like a woman, they'd say I sound like a cat, hah hah" (quoted in Heilbut, *Gospel Sound*, 117).

43. The growl is a sound he picked up from Louis Johnson, a "shouter" who joined the group in 1955. Jeter recalls, "Louis made me add this growl. I'd be switch-leading with him, and I didn't dare get smooth behind his part. I tried to make a little growl and then smooth it over. It ain't really my style, and

I don't like it." But, Heilbut reports, the public did, and this particular sound began to be picked up by R & B groups (Heilbut, *Gospel Sound*, 119).

44. See again n. 30, in which Jeter happily acknowledges the group's commercial connections. Tricia Rose deals with a later moment of African American music in which African-based procedures are wed to state-of-the-art technology in her *Black Noise: Rap Music and Black Culture in Contemporary America* (Hanover, N.H.: Wesleyan University Press, 1994). Such practices challenge received notions that equate "authenticity" with acoustical purity.

45. Johannes de Grocheo, *De musica*, trans. Albert Seay (Colorado Springs: Colorado College Music Press, 1974).

46. Lydia Goehr, *The Imaginary Museum of Musical Works* (Oxford: Oxford University Press, 1992), 243.


## CHAPTER 2: THINKING BLUES

1. Donald Tovey, "The Main Stream of Music," in *The Main Stream of Music and Other Essays* (Cleveland: Meridian Books, 1959).

2. Leonard B. Meyer, *Music, the Arts, and Ideas* (Chicago: University of Chicago Press, 1967), chapters 6–9.

3. LeRoi Jones (now Amiri Baraka), *Blues People: The Negro Experience in White America and the Music That Developed From It* (New York: Morrow Quill, 1963).

4. Albert Murray, *Stomping the Blues* (New York: Viking, 1976), 126.

5. One of the most enlightening overviews in recent years is Francis Davis, *The History of the Blues: The Roots, the Music, the People from Charley Patton to Robert Cray* (New York: Hyperion, 1995).

6. See Arthur Schlesinger Jr., *The Disuniting of America: Reflections on a Multicultural Society* (New York: Norton, 1991), for arguments denying the African presence in African American practices in general.

7. Jones, *Blues People*, 66, and Lawrence W. Levine, *Black Culture and Black Consciousness: Afro-American Folk Thought from Slavery to Freedom* (Oxford: Oxford University Press, 1977), 221 and 223.

8. Gunther Schuller, *Early Jazz: Its Roots and Musical Development* (Oxford: Oxford University Press, 1968); Olly Wilson, "The Significance of the Relationship between Afro-American Music and West African Music," *Black Perspective in Music* 2 (1974): 3–22; Christopher Small, *Music of the Common*

*Tongue: Survival and Celebration in Afro-American Music* (London: John Calder, 1987); Henry Louis Gates Jr., *The Signifying Monkey; A Theory of African-American Literary Criticism* (Oxford: Oxford University Press, 1988); Peter van der Merwe, *Origins of the Popular Style* (Oxford: Oxford University Press, 1989); Paul Gilroy, *The Black Atlantic: Modernity and Double Consciousness* (Cambridge, Mass.: Harvard University Press, 1993); Samuel A. Floyd, Jr., *The Power of Black Music: Interpreting Its History from Africa to the United States* (Oxford: Oxford University Press, 1995).

9. Ernest Borneman, "The Roots of Jazz," in *Jazz: New Perspectives on the History of Jazz by Twelve of the World's Foremost Jazz Critics and Scholars*, ed. Nat Hentoff and Albert J. McCarthy (New York: Da Capo, 1959), 17.

10. Sterling Stuckey, *Slave Culture: Nationalist Theory and the Foundations of Black America* (Oxford: Oxford University Press, 1987), 25.

11. For instance, the seventeenth-century *ciaccona* was attributed sometimes to Peruvian Indians, sometimes to displaced Africans; Stephen Foster's songs present themselves as "artful" imitations of slave songs; and the hit tune in Bizet's *Carmen*, the "Habañera," was modeled after an African-based genre from Cuba. For a discussion of the *ciaccona*, see my "Music, the Pythagoreans, and the Body," in *Choreographing History*, ed. Susan Leigh Foster (Bloomington: Indiana University Press, 1995), 82–104; for more on Bizet's borrowings, see my *Georges Bizet: Carmen* (Cambridge: Cambridge University Press, 1993).

12. Murray, *Stomping the Blues*, 70. Although sometimes titled "blues," Handy's tunes were originally classified as rags on the sheet music (70, 81). See 139–40 for Handy's account of how he cobbled "St. Louis Blues" together out of various commercial elements.

13. Daphne Duval Harrison, *Black Pearls: Blues Queens of the 1920s* (New Brunswick: Rutgers University Press, 1988), 57–58.

14. Harrison, *Black Pearls*, 56. See also Murray, *Stomping*, chapter 11, for a discussion of the folk/art debate surrounding blues.

15. George Lipsitz, *Time Passages: Collective Memory and American Popular Music* (Minneapolis: University of Minnesota Press, 1990).

16. Harrison, *Black Pearls*, 35.

17. Houston Baker Jr., *Blues, Ideology, and Afro-American Literature: A Vernacular History* (Chicago: University of Chicago Press, 1984).

18. Recorded on January 14, 1925 (available in the *Smithsonian Collection of Classic Jazz*). The harmonium player, Fred Longshaw, introduces many very

tasty harmonic inflections within the basic blues structure, but I indicate only the basic schema in my diagram.

19. I am greatly indebted to Robert Walser for this discussion of blues conventions. In contrast to him, alas, I cannot pull out a guitar and demonstrate.

20. See Simon Frith and Howard Horne, *Art into Pop* (London: Methuen, 1987), 92.

21. The most thorough account of the material conditions surrounding these women appears in Harrison, *Black Pearls*.

22. Quoted in Harrison, *Black Pearls*, 44.

23. See Hazel Carby, "'It Jus Be's Dat Way Sometime': The Sexual Politics of Women's Blues," in *Unequal Sisters: A Multi-Cultural Reader in U.S. Women's History*, ed. Ellen Carol DuBois and Vicki L. Ruiz (New York: Routledge, 1990), 239; Harrison, *Black Pearls*. For a remarkable fictional exploration of this world, see also Toni Morrison's novel *Jazz* (New York: Alfred A. Knopf, 1992).

24. Carby argues that the black women responsible for literary works tended to minimize sexuality, which is why women's blues become such important documents. Women composers and musicians in the European art tradition too have often tried to minimize references to sexuality: in fact, many feminist musicologists were disconcerted by my discussions in *Feminine Endings*. I owe my serious concern with this repertory to Barbara Christian. When I was first beginning to work on issues involving women and music, I explained to Christian that women had only recently begun to deal explicitly with gender and sexuality in their music. To which she responded: "Ever hear of Bessie Smith?" I have never forgotten that lesson.

25. Carby, "It Jus Be's," 241 and 247. For the importance of joy and pleasure in black culture in general, see Gina Dent, "Black Pleasure, Black Joy: An Introduction," the essay that opens the forum of leading black theorists in *Black Popular Culture*, a project by Michele Wallace, ed. Gina Dent (Seattle: Bay Press, 1992), 1–20.

26. See bell hooks, "Selling Hot Pussy: Representations of Black Female Sexuality in the Cultural Marketplace," *Black Looks: Race and Representation* (Boston: South End Press, 1992), for a critique of several music videos featuring black women. For a discussion of this problem in music studies, see Robert Walser and Susan McClary, "Theorizing the Body in African-American Music," *Black Music Research Journal* 14 (1994): 75–84.

27. See Sander L. Gilman, "The Hottentot and the Prostitute: Toward an Iconography of Female Sexuality," and "Black Sexuality and Modern Consciousness," in his *Difference and Pathology: Stereotypes of Sexuality, Race, and Madness* (Ithaca: Cornell University Press, 1985).

28. Angela Davis, *Blues Legacies and Black Feminism: Gertrude "Ma" Rainey, Bessie Smith, and Billie Holiday* (New York: Pantheon, 1998).

29. Bessie Smith, "Thinking Blues," Demas Dean, cornet; Charlie Green, trombone; Fred Longshaw, piano (February 9, 1928, Columbia 14292-D).

30. See, for instance, Schuller, *Early Jazz:*, 241: "Her tragic early death was perhaps a less painful exit than a long decline into oblivion. For Bessie Smith was one of the great tragic figures, not only of jazz, but of her period." He then adds, "But Bessie Smith was a supreme artist, and as such her art transcends the particulars of life that informed that art." For an important warning against such romanticizing, see again the quotation from Albert Murray near the beginning of this chapter.

31. John Coltrane, quoted in Carby, "It Jus Be's," 242.

32. For an account of the relationship between Delta blues and urban electric blues, see Robert Palmer, *Deep Blues: A Musical and Cultural History of the Mississippi Delta* (New York: Penguin, 1982).

33. Robert Johnson, "Cross Road Blues" (San Antonio, November 27, 1936; Columbia 46222).

34. See the transcription and discussion in Dave Headlam, "Blues Transformations in the Music of Cream," *Understanding Rock: Essays in Musical Analysis*, ed. John Covach and Graeme M. Boone (New York: Oxford University Press, 1997), 62–69.

35. George Lipsitz, "White Desire: Remembering Robert Johnson," in *The Possessive Investment in Whiteness: How White People Profit from Identity Politics* (Philadelphia: Temple University Press, 1998), 118–38. My chapter was completed before I encountered Lipsitz's treatment, but we have talked about these issues over the course of many years. His influence on my work in this area cannot be overestimated.

For a significantly different appropriation of the Johnson legend, however, see Sherman Alexie, *Reservation Blues* (New York: Warner Books, 1995), in which Johnson's ghost bestows his guitar to Thomas Builds-the-Fire and Victor Joseph—both now famous as characters in the 1998 film *Smoke Signals*. Alexie plays ironically with the myth surrounding Johnson as he examines the poverty and attempts at cultural/spiritual survival in a contemporary Spokane Indian reservation.

36. Quoted in Simon Frith, *Sound Effects: Youth, Leisure, and the Politics of Rock'n'Roll* (New York: Pantheon, 1981), 15.

37. See Frith and Horne, *Art into Pop*, 73.

38. Ibid., 72, and Ian Chambers, *Urban Rhythms: Pop Music and Popular Culture* (New York: St. Martin's Press, 1985), 67.

39. John Lennon, quoted in Frith, *Art into Pop*, 81.

40. Eric Clapton, quoted in Geoffrey Stokes, "The Sixties," in *Rock of Ages: The Rolling Stone History of Rock 'n' Roll* (New York: Summit Press, 1986), 395.

41. See Stokes, "Sixties," 282–83: "But bitter as it was, the blues-vs.-trad battle was taking place in an extremely small pond. Recording contracts were rare, and purism—as that purist Eric Clapton, who quit the Yardbirds to join John Mayall when they grew too poppish, recalled—was a badge of honor: 'The blues musician is usually a fanatic; that's the common denominator among blues musicians, they're fanatics. In England, they're a lot more so 'cause they're divorced from the scene and don't really know where it's at. They don't know what it's like to be a blues musician in America like Mike Bloomfield does. They're all romantic about it and have a lot of ideals and notions. A lot of ego gets mixed into it and they think they're the only guys playing real music.'"

42. See Richard Leppert, *Music and Image: Domesticity, Ideology, and Sociocultural Formation in Eighteenth-Century England* (Cambridge: Cambridge University Press, 1989), and Linda Austern, "'Alluring the Auditorie to Effeminacie': Music and the English Renaissance Idea of the Feminine," *Music and Letters* 74 (1993): 343–54.

43. Philip Brett, "Musicality, Essentialism, and the Closet," *Queering the Pitch: The New Gay and Lesbian Musicology*, ed. Philip Brett, Elizabeth Wood, and Gary C. Thomas (New York: Routledge, 1994), 9–26.

44. Chambers, *Urban Rhythms*, 67.

45. See ibid., 20.

46. Keith Richards, "Well, This Is It," in liner notes for *Robert Johnson: The Complete Recordings* (Columbia/CBS Records, 1990), 22.

47. Eric Clapton, "Discovering Robert Johnson," in liner notes for *Robert Johnson*, 22.

48. Ibid., 22.

49. See Milton Babbitt, "Who Cares If You Listen?," *High Fidelity Magazine* 8, no. 2 (February 1958): 126. See my "Terminal Prestige: The Case of Avant-Garde Music Composition," *Cultural Critique* 12 (1989): 57–81.

50. Cream, "Crossroads," reissued on *Wheels of Fire* (Polygram, 1976). This performance was recorded live at the Fillmore. Clapton's much-publicized identification with Johnson in general and this song in particular inspired the title of one of his biographies: Michael Schumacher, *Crossroads: The Life and Music of Eric Clapton* (New York: Hyperion, 1995).

51. Robert Walser has shown that this particular fusion prepared the way for the literal incorporation of Vivaldian passagework into heavy metal. See *Running with the Devil: Power, Gender, and Madness in Heavy Metal Music* (Hanover, N.H.: Wesleyan University Press, 1993).

52. Gregory Bateson has written on the convention of climax in Western cultural artifacts. See *Steps to an Ecology of Mind* (New York: Ballantine Books, 1972), 113. I once attended a performance by Joe Turner's blues band in which Turner delivered his famous shouts, the piano player boogie-woogie, the sax player a series of alienated posthop squawks, and the white guitarist a narrative excursion into greater and greater frustration with a final spray-down release, followed by Turner shouting out a verse in conclusion. This sequence occurred without fail on every number in the concert.

53. See also Lipsitz, "White Desire." For a formal analysis of Cream's performance of "Crossroads," see Headlam, "Blues Transformations in the Music of Cream," 69–72. Once again, Headlam's transcriptions prove very useful.

54. Dave Morse, quoted in Chambers, *Urban Rhythms*, 117. Chambers comments: "Employing the accusation of 'commercialism', black performers were compared unfavourably to what were referred to as the 'blue-eyed white soul singers' . . . The soul and R & B strains of Janis Joplin, Rod Stewart, Joe Cocker and Van Morrison were praised, while Ray Charles and Aretha Franklin, not to mention the unredeemable Tamla Motown stable . . . were accused of decaying in the swamps of a commercial jungle" (118).

55. Mick Jagger said of the appropriation of black music: "These legendary characters wouldn't mean a light commercially today if groups were not going round Britain doing their numbers" (quoted in Stokes, "Sixties," 283). From the other side, Muddy Waters said of Jagger: "He took my music. But he gave me my name" (quoted in Chambers, *Urban Rhythms*, 69).

## CHAPTER 3: WHAT WAS TONALITY?

1. See Raymond Williams, *Marxism and Literature* (Oxford: Oxford University Press, 1977), 128–35. For a discussion of the difficulty of understanding our own structures of feeling, see my *Rap, Minimalism, and Structures of Time in Late Twentieth-Century Culture* (Lincoln: University of Nebraska Press, 1999).

2. For an excellent account of these documents, see Mark Evan Bonds, *Wordless Rhetoric: Musical Form and the Metaphor of the Oration* (Cambridge, Mass: Harvard University Press, 1991). Bonds approaches many of the issues addressed in this chapter through the theoretical treatises of the eighteenth century. See also Joel Lester, *Compositional Theory in the Eighteenth Century* (Cambridge, Mass.: Harvard University Press, 1992).

3. Leonard Ratner, *Classic Music: Expression, Form, and Style* (New York: Schirmer, 1980), and Wye Jamison Allanbrook, *Rhythmic Gesture in Mozart* (Chicago: University of Chicago Press, 1983).

4. For discussions of musical autonomy, see Janet Wolff, "The Ideology of Autonomous Art," foreword to *Music and Society: The Politics of Composition, Performance, and Reception*, ed. Richard Leppert and Susan McClary (Cambridge: Cambridge University Press, 1987), 1–12, and Lydia Goehr, *The Imaginary Museum of Musical Works* (Oxford: Oxford University Press, 1992). For an excellent account of the social conditions within which the ideology of artistic autonomy developed, see Martha Woodmansee, *The Author, Art, and the Market: Rereading the History of Aesthetics* (New York: Columbia University Press, 1994).

5. See Carolyn Abbate, *Unsung Voices: Opera and Musical Narrative in the Nineteenth Century* (Princeton: Princeton University Press, 1991), xiv. Abbate is especially concerned to delimit the use of narrative approaches to instrumental music; my project takes a very different position with respect to both metaphor in general and narrative in particular.

6. For more on metaphor as an active producer of cultural knowledge, see George Lakoff and Mark Johnson, *Metaphors We Live By* (Chicago: University of Chicago Press, 1980); Mark Johnson, *The Body in the Mind: The Bodily Basis of Meaning, Imagination, and Reason* (Chicago: University of Chicago Press, 1987); Paul Ricoeur, "The Function of Fiction in Shaping Reality," in *A Ricoeur Reader: Reflection and Imagination*, ed. Mario J. Valdés (Toronto: University of Toronto Press, 1991), 117–36; and Robert Walser, "The Body in the

Music: Epistemology and Musical Semiotics," *College Music Symposium* 31 (1991): 117–26.

7. For illuminating comparisons between modern European notions of time and those of others, see Judith Becker and Alton Becker, "A Musical Icon: Power and Meaning in Javanese Gamelan Music," in *The Sign in Music and Literature*, ed. Wendy Steiner (Austin: University of Texas Press, 1981), 203–15; John S. Mbiti, "The Concept of Time," in his *African Religions and Philosophy*, 2d ed. (Oxford: Heinemann, 1989), 15–28; and Donald M. Lowe, *History of Bourgeois Perception* (Chicago: University of Chicago Press, 1982); Johannes Fabian, *Time and the Other* (New York: Columbia University Press, 1983). For more on Glass, see chapter 5.

8 Heinrich Schenker, *Free Composition*, trans. and ed. Ernst Oster (New York: Longman, 1979).

9. Robert Morgan, "Musical Time/Musical Space," *Critical Inquiry* 7 (1980): 527–38, and Jean-François Lyotard, "Several Silences," trans. Joseph Maier, *Driftworks*, ed. Roger McKean (New York: Semiotext(e), 1984), 95–98.

10. See the discussions in Terry Eagleton, *The Ideology of the Aesthetic* (Oxford: Basil Blackwell, 1990); Friedrich Kittler, *Discourse Networks 1800/1900*, trans. Michael Metteer and Chris Cullens (Stanford: Stanford University Press, 1990); and Charles Taylor, *Sources of the Self: The Making of the Modern Identity* (Cambridge, Mass.: Harvard University Press, 1989). Taylor argues compellingly that we not discard this version of the self in our postmodern haste to rid ourselves of outmoded conventions.

11. See my "Gender Ambiguities and Erotic Excess in Seventeenth-Century Venetian Opera," in *Actualizing Absence: Performance, Visuality, Writing*, ed. Mark Franko and Annette Richards (Hanover, N.H.: Wesleyan University Press, 1999), and "Second-Hand Emotions: Toward a History of Western Interiority in Music," *Contemporary Sound Arts: Essays in Sound* 3 (1996): 92–104.

12. See the classic parodies by Benedetto Marcello and Joseph Addison in Oliver Strunk, ed., *Source Readings in Music History* (New York: Norton, 1950), 511–31. Robert Freeman, "Opera without Drama" (Ph.D. diss., Princeton University, 1967), Joseph Kerman, *Opera as Drama*, rev. ed. (Berkeley and Los Angeles: University of California Press, 1988), chapter 3.

13. See Norman Bryson, "The Legible Body: LeBrun," in *Word and Image: French Painting of the Ancien Régime* (Cambridge: Cambridge University Press, 1981), chapter 2.

14. See Norbert Elias, *The Court Society*, trans. Edmund Jephcott (New York: Pantheon, 1983). For an extensive discussion of how absolutist politics influenced the details of music composition, see my "Unruly Passions and Courtly Dances: Technologies of the Body in Baroque Music," in *Embodying Power in Seventeenth- and Eighteenth-Century France*, ed. Sara Melzer and Kathryn Norberg (Berkeley and Los Angeles: University of California Press, 1998).

15. For more on the politically motivated encroachment of reason over behavior during this period, see Michel Foucault, *Discipline and Punish: The Birth of the Prison*, trans. Alan Sheridan (New York: Vintage Books, 1979).

16. Johann Mattheson, *Der vollkommene Capellmeister* (Hamburg, 1739), trans. Ernest C. Harriss (Ann Arbor: UMI, 1981).

17. See chapter 1. Such enactments sometimes occur (though rarely) in the eighteenth century: see my discussion of Bach's Brandenburg No. 5 in "The Blasphemy of Talking Politics during Bach Year," in *Music and Society: The Politics of Composition, Performance, and Reception*, ed. Richard Leppert and Susan McClary (Cambridge: Cambridge University Press, 1987), 21–41.

18. The pivot takes place by way of the common pitch, G—tonic in G minor and mediant in E♭. Although this juxtaposition of I and iii falls out of favor by the later part of the eighteenth century, it occurs frequently in opera seria. The shared tone establishes in the strongest possible manner the principal key's third degree, which Schenker regards as the opening position for major-key background descents and which also functioned as the second most important pitch (after the tonic) in ionian-based structures. A great deal of work remains to be done on the history of tonal strategies, once we can accept them as having a history.

19. For a discussion of how Vivaldian models were appropriated by metal musicians, see Robert Walser, *Running with the Devil: Power, Gender, and Madness in Heavy Metal Music* (Hanover, N.H.: Wesleyan University Press, 1993), chapter 3.

20. See Paul Ricoeur, *Time and Narrative*, vol. 1, trans. Kathleen McLaughlin and David Pellauer (Chicago: University of Chicago Press, 1984).

21. So-called rage arias often appeared in operas and oratorios of the day, offering opportunities for virtuosity and demonstrating the ways in which rationality and anger could be reconciled. The most familiar to modern listeners is probably "Why Do the Nations" in Handel's *Messiah*, and the aria by

Griselda discussed earlier in this chapter also incorporates many stereotypical elements of rage.

22. The setting of the *Passamezzo Antico* most familiar to contemporary listeners is the first strain of "Greensleeves," in which the opening tonic moves directly to ♭VII—a harmonic progression that supports the descent from $\hat{5}$ to $\hat{4}$ in the controlling structural line. The same structural line is harmonized differently in the chorus ("Greensleeves was all my joy . . . "), which begins on III and then moves rather more elegantly to ♭VII. See my "The Transition from Modal to Tonal Organization in the Works of Monteverdi" (Ph.D. diss. Harvard University, 1976).

23. See the discussion of Vivaldi's reception in Michael Talbot's entry on Vivaldi in *The New Grove Dictionary of Music and Musicians*, vol. 20, ed. Stanley Sadie (London: MacMillan, 1980).

24. See, for instance, Adorno's account of Bach's fugues in "Bach Defended against His Devotees," in *Prisms*, trans. Samuel Weber and Shierry Weber (Cambridge, Mass.: MIT Press, 1981), 133–46.

25. See Norbert Elias, *The History of Manners: The Civilizing Process*, vol. 1, trans. Edmund Jephcott (New York: Pantheon Books, 1978), chapter 1.

26. Eagleton, *Ideology of the Aesthetic*.

27. Maynard Solomon, *Mozart* (Cambridge, Mass.: Harvard University Press, 1995).

28. For a more detailed reading of the "Prague" Symphony along these same lines, see my "Narratives of Bourgeois Subjectivity in Mozart's 'Prague' Symphony," in *Understanding Narrative*, ed. Peter Rabinowitz and James Phelan (Columbus: Ohio State University Press, 1994), 65–98.

29. See "Blasphemy of Talking Politics during Bach Year," 13–63, and Susan McClary, "A Musical Dialectic from the Enlightenment: Mozart's Piano Concerto in G Major, K. 453, Movement 2," *Cultural Critique* 4 (1986): 129–69.

# CHAPTER 4: THE REFUGE
## OF COUNTERCONVENTION

1. This ideologically motivated distrust of the means of communication—not simply of the messages they carry—recurred in the years following the 1960s. Both moments witnessed a retreat from overt politics to methods we

now theorize as deconstruction. For a diagnosis of our own intellectual time, see *In Defense of History: Marxism and the Postmodern Agenda*, ed. Ellen Meiksins Wood and John Bellamy Foster (New York: Monthly Review Press, 1997). For a discussion comparing the cultural strategies of the two moments, see Vijay Mishra, *The Gothic Sublime* (Albany: State University of New York Press, 1994), especially chapters 1 and 2. The cultural artifacts and philosophical stances of both periods foreground experiences of discontinuity and rupture, and they revel in the rubble of a defeated rationality.

2. See, for instance, Carl Dahlhaus, *The Idea of Absolute Music*, trans. Roger Lustig (Chicago: University of Chicago Press, 1989), and John Neubauer, *The Emancipation of Music from Language: Departure from Mimesis in Eighteenth-Century Aesthetics* (New Haven: Yale University Press, 1986).

3. Norbert Elias, *The History of Manners: The Civilizing Process*, vol. 1, trans. Edmund Jephcott (New York: Pantheon Books, 1978), chapter 1.

4. Klaus Doerner, *Madmen and the Bourgeoisie: A Social History of Insanity and Psychiatry*, trans. Joachim Neugroschel and Jean Steinberg (Oxford: Basil Blackwell, 1981), 195.

5. J. N. Forkel, *On Johann Sebastian Bach's Life, Genius, and Works* (1802), trans. Mr. Stephenson (1808), in *The Bach Reader*, ed. Hans T. David and Arthur Mendel (New York: Norton, 1945), 295–353; *E. T. A. Hoffmann: Kreisleriana, The Poet and the Composer, Musical Writings*, ed. David Charlton, trans. Martyn Clarke (Cambridge: Cambridge University Press, 1989).

6. Friedrich Kittler, *Discourse Networks, 1800/1900*, trans. Michael Metteer (Stanford: Stanford University Press, 1990).

7. For a superb analysis of this crucial cultural moment, see Martha Woodmansee, *The Author, Art, and the Market: Rereading the History of Aesthetics* (New York: Columbia University Press, 1994).

8. Recall, for instance, the controversies surrounding the reception of Liszt, in which these attempts at gender-based policing become remarkably explicit. See the picture reproduced in Piero Weiss and Richard Taruskin, eds., *Music in the Western World: A History in Documents* (New York: Schirmer Books, 1984), 364, and imagine that the men catching the swooning women would have preferred thinking about formal diagrams. I am grateful to Marischka Olech Hopcroft, whose dissertation research on Liszt has unearthed dozens of anti-woman pronouncements.

9. Carl Dahlhaus, *Nineteenth-Century Music*, trans. J. Bradford Robinson (Berkeley and Los Angeles: University of California Press, 1989), 313.

10. For an insightful examination of this concept and its history, see Rose Rosengard Subotnik, "Toward a Deconstruction of Structural Listening: A Critique of Schoenberg, Adorno, and Stravinsky," in *Deconstructive Variations: Music and Reason in Western Society* (Minneapolis: University of Minnesota Press, 1996), 148–76.

11. Stephen Rumph, "A Kingdom Not of This World: The Political Context of E. T. A. Hoffmann's Beethoven Criticism," *19th-Century Music* 19, no. 1 (Summer 1995): 50–67. For English translations of Hoffmann's work, see again n. 5.

12. Rumph, "A Kingdom Not of This World," 59.

13. Sanna Pederson has examined the polemics surrounding these issues in nineteenth-century Germany in her dissertation and a series of important articles. See, for instance, her "A. B. Marx, Berlin Concert Life, and German National Identity," *19th-Century Music* 18, no. 2 (Fall 1994): 87–107.

14. Of course, Wagner's Senta is scarcely less selfless than Griselda; she merely attaches herself to an outsider instead of to the king. As women connected with Marxist and civil rights causes have often discovered, liberation movements do not always acknowledge gender as an issue.

15. See Susan McClary, "The Blasphemy of Talking Politics during Bach Year," in *Music and Society: The Politics of Composition, Performance, and Reception*, ed. Richard Leppert and Susan McClary (Cambridge: Cambridge University Press, 1987), 13–62, and "A Dialectic from the Enlightenment: Mozart's Piano Concerto in G Major, K. 453, Movement 2," *Cultural Critique* 4 (1986): 129–69.

16. For an account of jazz that brings the attendant controversies to light again, see Robert Walser, ed., *Keeping Time: Readings in Jazz History* (New York: Oxford University Press, 1998).

17. To date, my most infamous statement has to do with Beethoven's Ninth Symphony—a statement quoted out of context not only in musicological criticism but in places as unlikely as *Entertainment Weekly* and *Reader's Digest*. For the offending passage, see chapter 5 of my *Feminine Endings: Music, Gender, and Sexuality* (Minneapolis: University of Minnesota Press, 1991), 128–29.

18. Joseph Kerman, "Beethoven: The Single Journey," *The Hudson Review* 5 (1952): 32–55.

19. V. Kofi Agawu, *Playing with Signs: A Semiotic Interpretation of Classic Music* (Princeton: Princeton University Press, 1991), chapter 6.

20. Adorno's various writings and jottings concerning Beethoven have just been collected and published. See Adorno, *Beethoven: The Philosophy of Music*, ed. Rolf Teidemann, trans. Edmund Jephcott (Stanford: Stanford University Press, 1998); Rose Rosengard Subotnik, *Developing Variations: Style and Ideology in Western Music* (Minneapolis: University of Minnesota Press, 1991), especially chapter 2, "Adorno's Diagnosis of Beethoven's Late Style: Early Symptom of a Fatal Condition."

21. Petrarch, "Mia benigna fortuna," *Rime sparse* 332.

22. See my "Pitches, Expression, Ideology: An Exercise in Mediation," *Enclitic* 7 (1983): 76–86. See also Thomas K. Nelson, "The Fantasy of Absolute Music" (Ph.D. diss., Minneapolis, University of Minnesota, 1998), which examines submediant strategies throughout the nineteenth century.

23. Joseph Kerman, *The Beethoven Quartets* (New York: Norton, 1966), 277.

24. Agawu, *Playing with Signs*, 120–21.

25. Recall, for instance, the ambiguity in Vivaldi between self-contained and dynamic cycles. Bach and Mozart both exploit from time to time the potential for circles of fifths to project a terrifying sense of free-fall: see the middle of Bach's Brandenburg No. 5, movement 1, or the development section of Mozart's Symphony No. 40 in G minor.

26. Agawu, *Playing with Signs*, 121.

27. Jacques Attali, *Noise: The Political Economy of Music*, trans. Brian Massumi (Minneapolis: University of Minnesota Press, 1985), 11.

28. Leo Treitler, "History, Criticism, and Beethoven's Ninth Symphony," in *Music and the Historical Imagination* (Cambridge, Mass.: Harvard University Press, 1989), especially 25–28.

29. Ross Chambers, *Story and Situation: Narrative Seduction and the Power of Fiction* (Minneapolis: University of Minnesota Press, 1984), chapter 1.

30. Peter Middleton, *The Inward Gaze: Masculinity and Subjectivity in Modern Culture* (New York: Routledge, 1992).

31. Hal Foster, "The Expressive Fallacy," in *Recodings: Art, Spectacle, Cultural Politics* (Seattle: Bay Press, 1985), 60–63.

32. Adorno draws such connections repeatedly throughout his work. See, for instance, the following passages in *Aesthetic Theory*, trans. Robert Hullot-Kentor (Minneapolis: University of Minnesota Press, 1997): "[D]issonance, the seal of everything modern, gives access to the alluringly sensuous by transfiguring it into its antithesis, pain" (15). "Art . . . has always desired disso-

nance. . . . Dissonance is effectively expression. . . . [E]xpression is scarcely to be conceived except as the expression of suffering. . . . " (110).

33. See the discussion of musical depth in Jean-François Lyotard, "Several Silences," in *Driftworks*, ed. Roger McKean (New York: Semiotext(e), 1984), 95–98. See also Fredric Jameson, *Postmodernism, or, The Cultural Logic of Late Capitalism* (Durham, N.C.: Duke University Press, 1991), chapter 1 on depth—or lack thereof—in Warhol.

34. See Robert Schumann, "A Symphony by Berlioz," *Neue Zeitschrift für Musik* (July and August 1835), translated in Edward T. Cone, *Berlioz: Fantastic Symphony* (New York: Norton, 1971), 220–48; Allen Forte, *The Harmonic Organization of The Rite of Spring* (New Haven: Yale University Press, 1978); Matthew Brown, "'Little Wing': A Study in Musical Cognition," in *Understanding Rock: Essays in Musical Analysis*, ed. John Covach and Graeme M. Boone (New York: Oxford University Press, 1997), 155–70.

35. See Richard Taruskin, *Stravinsky and the Russian Traditions: A Biography of the Works through* Mavra (Berkeley and Los Angeles: University of California Press, 1996), *passim*.

## CHAPTER 5: REVELING IN THE RUBBLE: THE POSTMODERN CONDITION

1. Robert Morgan, *Twentieth Century Music* (New York: Norton, 1991), 486–89; Leonard B. Meyer, *Music, the Arts, and Ideas* (Chicago: University of Chicago Press, 1967), chapters 6–9. I discussed the image of the main stream as it circulates within musicology in chapter 2.

2. Theodor W. Adorno, "Cultural Criticism and Society," in *Prisms*, trans. Samuel Weber and Shierry Weber (Cambridge, Mass.: MIT Press, 1981), 34. See, however, Adorno's *Quasi una fantasia: Essays on Modern Music*, trans. Rodney Livingstone (London: Verso, 1992), for his attempts to come to terms with the music that was, in fact, written after Auschwitz.

3. Fredric Jameson, "Postmodernism and Consumer Culture," in *The Anti-Aesthetic: Essays on Postmodern Culture*, ed. Hal Foster (Port Townsend, Wash.: Bay Press, 1983), 113–15; for an extended treatment of the ideas presented in this essay, see also his *Postmodernism, or, The Cultural Logic of Late Capitalism* (Durham, N.C.: Duke University Press, 1991).

4. Jean Baudrillard, "Simulacra and Simulations," in *Jean Baudrillard: Selected Writings*, ed. Mark Poster (Stanford: Stanford University Press, 1988), 166–84.

5. See the discussion of the prohibition against representation in Jean-François Lyotard, *The Postmodern Condition: A Report on Knowledge*, trans. Geoff Bennington and Brian Massumi (Minneapolis: University of Minnesota Press, 1984), 78–82. For a provocative discussion of music history through Cage, see "Several Silences," in his *Driftworks*, trans. Joseph Maier (New York: Semiotext(e), 1984), 91–110.

6. David Del Tredici, especially *In Memory of a Summer Day* (1980) and *Final Alice* (1981). See John Rockwell, "The Return of Tonality, the Orchestral Audience and the Danger of Success," in *All American Music: Composition in the Late Twentieth Century* (New York: Alfred A. Knopf, 1983), 71–83.

7. Philip Glass, "Opening," *Glassworks* (CBS Records, 1982; score: Bryn Mawr, Penn.: Dunvagen Music Publishers, Inc., 1982).

8. Michael Nyman's score for Jane Campion's *The Piano* (1993), for instance, makes use of these patterns in a film meant to depict the nineteenth century.

9. Glass's music is beginning to receive the detailed study it deserves; see, for instance, John Richardson, *Singing Archaeology: Philip Glass's* Akhnaten (Hanover, N.H.: Wesleyan University Press, 1999). Robert Fink is now completing a book concerning minimalist music for University of California Press. See also my *Rap, Minimalism, and Structures of Time in Late Twentieth-Century Music* (Lincoln: University of Nebraska Press, 1999).

10. Teresa de Lauretis, "Desire in Narrative," in *Alice Doesn't: Feminism, Semiotics, Cinema* (Bloomington: Indiana University Press, 1984), 103–57. The phrase "narrative with a vengeance" comes from the concluding sentence of her essay.

11. John Zorn, *Spillane* (Elektra/Asylum/Nonesuch, 1987).

12. V. Kofi Agawu, *Playing with Signs: A Semiotic Interpretation of Classic Music* (Princeton: Princeton University Press, 1991). See again chapter 4.

13. See Jean Baudrillard, "The Ecstasy of Communication," in *Anti-Aesthetic*, ed. Foster, 126–34. E. Ann Kaplan uses imagery of this sort to theorize the music videos on MTV, though she neglects to mention the level of coherence contributed by the songs, which anchor the visuals in effect. See her *Rocking around the Clock: Music Television, Postmodernism, and Consumer Culture* (New York: Methuen, 1987).

14. Zorn, *Spillane*, liner notes.

15. The sound of rain on urban streets constitutes a standard convention of the *noir* soundtrack, despite the desert climate of Los Angeles. Affective considerations here prevail over reality.

16. Recall, for instance, Berlioz's *Symphonie fantastique, Roméo et Juliette*, or *La Damnation de Faust*. Berlioz arranges his moments of musical elaboration much as his French operatic predecessors did their interpolated divertissements.

17. Zorn, "John Zorn on His Music," liner notes, *Spillane*.

18. Ibid.

19. Andreas Huyssen, *After the Great Divide: Modernism, Mass Culture, Postmodernism* (Bloomington: Indiana University, 1986).

20. John Zorn, "Road Runner," on Guy Klucevsek's *Transylvanian Softwear* (John Marks Records 4, 1994); *The Big Gundown: John Zorn Plays the Music of Ennio Morricone* (New York: Icon Records, 1986).

21. Ellie Hisama, "Postcolonialism on the Make: The Music of John Mellencamp, David Bowie and John Zorn," *Popular Music*, vol. 12, no. 2 (1993): 91–104.

22. A useful summary of the debate appears in Denise Hamilton, "Zorn's 'Garden' Sprouts Discontent," *Los Angeles Times*, Calendar Section (August 15, 1994), 9.

23. John Zorn, quoted in Hamilton, "Zorn's 'Garden' Sprouts Discontent." Zorn cites as his models for violent imagery literary theorist Georges Bataille and photographer Joel-Peter Witkin. He might also argue that the Western avant-garde since the mid-nineteenth century has often looked to the works of Sade for inspiration. See the insightful discussion of Sade as a touchstone of Modernism and recent reassessments in Robert Darnton, "The Real Marquis," *New York Review of Books*, vol. 46, no. 1 (January 14, 1999): 19–24.

24. Zorn, quoted in Hamilton, "Zorn's 'Garden' Sprouts Discontent."

25. Michael Dorf, quoted in Hamilton, "Zorn's 'Garden' Sprouts Discontent."

26. Del Tredici's *In Memory of a Summer Day* (1980) includes a passage scored for bullwhips and police sirens, labeled as the moment when Alice discovers her true desires; John Adams's *Harmonielehre* (1985) begins with what the composer describes on the liner notes as "very violent and shocking"—a series of pounding E-minor chords that helped to exorcize a period during which he had difficulty composing. The chords and their violence served to launch him again into narrative.

27. De Lauretis, "Desire in Narrative," 132.

28. Relatively little has been written about disco until recently. See Richard Dyer, "In Defence of Disco," in *On Record: Rock, Pop, and the Written Word*, ed. Simon Frith and Andrew Goodwin (New York: Pantheon Press, 1990), 410–18. See also John Gill, *Queer Noises* (Minneapolis: University of Minnesota Press, 1995). Mitchell Morris is now editing a collection on the music of disco for University of California Press.

29. Prince, "Kiss," *Parade* (Warner, 1986); the album gives the Artist's father, John L. Nelson, credit for co-writing the song. The song was originally intended for Mazarati, and David Z of Mazarati participated in its genesis and arrangement. Both David Z and the Artist perceived the song as bizarre and shelved it repeatedly before it finally appeared on *Parade*. It became a No. 1 single.

For another reading of the song, see Robert Walser, "Prince as Queer Poststructuralist," *Popular Music and Society* 18, no. 2 (1994): 79–90. Rob and I developed our reading of "Kiss" together for a talk we delivered at the International Association for the Study of Popular Music Conference in Paris, 1989. I no longer have a clear sense of who contributed what to this particular interpretation, but I can say that I could never have addressed popular music *at all* without Rob's influence and greater knowledge.

30. The Artist appropriated female cheesecake imagery even more obviously on the cover of his 1988 album *Lovesexy*. He has paid dearly for these transgressions, which have raised storms of controversy over his sexuality. The public does not uniformly recognize the ironies celebrated by poststructuralist theorists.

31. See my comparison between the Artist's constructions and those of Francesco Cavalli in *Il Giasone* in "Gender Ambiguities and Erotic Excess in Seventeenth-Century Venetian Opera," in *Actualizing Absence: Performance, Visuality, Writing*, ed. Mark Franko and Annette Richards (Hanover, N.H.: Wesleyan University Press, 1999). See also the discussion of Stradella's *La Susanna* in chapter 1.

32. "Gett Off," "Insatiable," and "Cream," *Diamonds and Pearls* (Paisley Park/Warner, 1991); "Electric Chair," *Batman* (Warner, 1989).

33. "Kiss" apparently raised a sufficient challenge to masculinity that its cover by Tom Jones and the Art of Noise did everything possible to reinscribe it with traditional phallic symbols: Jones's hilarious video fills the screen with

cartoon images of thrusting objects. Returning to the original video after viewing the cover makes the austere, uncompromising weirdness of the Artist's vision all the more striking.

34. This notion of gender as performance is most closely identified with Judith Butler, *Gender Trouble: Feminism and the Subversion of Identity* (New York: Routledge, 1990).

35. Arthur Kroker and David Cook, *The Postmodern Scene: Excremental Culture and Hyper-Aesthetics* (New York: St. Martin's Press, 1986), 21.

36. k.d. lang, *Ingenue* (Sire Records, 1992). *Absolute Torch and Twang* was released in 1989, also by Sire.

37. Tricia Rose, *Black Noise: Rap Music and Black Culture in Contemporary America* (Hanover, N.H.: Wesleyan University Press, 1994), chapter 3.

38. "The Princess of the Posse: Queen Latifah's *Ladies First*," panel on the study, analysis, and criticism of popular music, joint meeting of the American Musicological Society, Society for Music Theory, and Society for Ethnomusicology, Oakland, 1990.

39. The greatest controversies over rap have focused on 2 Live Crew, a group whose somewhat puerile rhymes became a cause célèbre that eventually drew in defenders such as Henry Louis Gates Jr.; Professor Griff, the spokesperson for NWA, ultimately fired for his outrageous statements; and Ice-T, whose "Cop Killer" raised a storm of protest that led to the number's removal from his heavy-metal album, *Body Count* (Sire, 1992). Ice-T has emerged as a surprisingly articulate cultural figure. See his *The Ice Opinion*, as told to Heidi Siegmund (New York: St. Martin's Press, 1994).

40. Public Enemy, *Apocalypse 91: The Enemy Strikes Black* (Sony, 1991).

41. The only serious treatment of rap *as music* is Robert Walser, "Rhythm, Rhyme, and Rhetoric in the Music of Public Enemy," *Ethnomusicology* 39 (1995): 193–217. My reading of "Nighttrain" owes a great deal to his detailed analysis of Public Enemy's "Fight the Power" and his arguments concerning Chuck D.

42. Jameson, "Postmodernism and Consumer Society," 115–16.

43. Fredric Jameson, *The Prison-House of Language: A Critical Account of Structuralism and Russian Formalism* (Princeton: Princeton University Press, 1972), i.

44. In my *Rap, Minimalism, and Structures of Time,* I offer few answers but principally examine the difficulties of explaining even the most obvious

conventions of present-day musical practice and some of the strands that must be factored in. We have not even begun to tell the story of twentieth-century music.

45. See Jocelyne Guilbault, *Zouk: World Music in the West Indies* (Chicago: University of Chicago Press, 1993); George Lipsitz, *Dangerous Crossroads: Popular Music, Postmodernism, and the Poetics of Place* (London: Verso, 1994); and Timothy D. Taylor, *Global Pop: World Music, World Markets* (New York: Routledge, 1997).

# INDEX

Abbate, Carolyn, 184n5

*Absolute Torch and Twang* (lang), 157

absolutism (French), 70, 81, 93, 95, 100, 101, 102, 104, 111, 115, 185n13, 186n14

Adams, John, 193n26; *Harmonielehre*, 193n26

Addison, Joseph, 69, 185n12

Adorno, Theodor W., 7, 114, 119, 128, 139, 167, 174n15, 187n24, 189n10, 190n20, 190–91n32, 191n2

*Affektenlehre*, 72, 73, 115

Africa: cultural practices of, 22, 24, 28, 34–36, 45, 159, 160, 178n6, 185n7; diaspora from, 24, 34, 35; popular musics of, 33; religious practices of, 24, 28, 52

Agawu, Kofi, 119–33, 135, 145, 189n19, 190nn24,26, 192n12

Alexie, Sherman, 181n35; *Reservation Blues*, 181n35

Allanbrook, Wye Jamison, 65, 172n5, 184n3

Anderson, Laurie, xii; "O Superman," xii

*Apocalypse 91: The Enemy Strikes Black* (Public Enemy), 161–66, 195n40

Arcadelt, Jacques, 175n21

arcadia, 123, 143

aria, 80, 122, 186n21; ABB′, 17–19, 72; da capo (ABA), 17, 18, 70–79, 95, 175n22

Armstrong, Louis, 39

Art of Noise, 194–95n33; "Kiss," 194–95n33

atonality, 116, 141

Attali, Jacques, 128, 190n27

*Aufklärung*, 72. *See also* Enlightenment

Austern, Linda, 182n42

authenticity, 37, 43, 52–60, 95, 144, 152–53, 160, 168, 178n44

autonomy: aesthetic, 2, 7, 66, 113, 114, 117, 134, 137, 169, 184n4. *See also* subjectivity: autonomous

Babbitt, Milton, 56, 136, 183n49

Bach, Carl Philipp Emanuel, 112

Bach, Johann Sebastian, xi, 10, 22, 30, 64, 69, 83, 94–101, 102, 105, 107, 112, 116, 117, 153, 168, 175n23, 186n17, 187nn24,29, 188n5, 189n15, 190n25; Brandenburg Concerto No. 5, 116, 175n23, 186n17, 190n25; Partita in D Major, 94, 96–101, 102, 107, 116

Baker, Ginger, 56

Baker, Houston, Jr., 39, 179n17

Baker, Josephine, 45

Text:  11/15 Granjon
Display:  Granjon
Composition:  Impressions Book and Journal Services, Inc.
Printing and binding:  BookCrafters
Music:  Rolf Wulfsberg